D1452671

Ethics and Religion
in a Pluralistic Age

Ethics and Religion in a Pluralistic Age

Collected Essays

Brian Hebblethwaite

T&T CLARK
EDINBURGH

T&T CLARK LTD
59 GEORGE STREET
EDINBURGH EH2 2LQ
SCOTLAND

First published 1997

ISBN 0 567 08551 1 HB
0 567 08570 8 PB

British Library Cataloguing-in-Publication Data
A catalogue record for this book is available from the British Library

Typeset by Waverley Typesetters, Galashiels
Printed and bound in Great Britain by Bookcraft, Avon

For Emma

Contents

Introduction

I have revised and brought together here twelve pieces, five of them previously unpublished, which bear on the many-sided theme of ethics and religion in a pluralistic age.

The six essays which form Part One reflect my long-standing conviction that ethics and doctrine belong together and that the very nature as well as the distinctiveness of the Christian way is bound up with and depends upon the truth of Christian doctrine. But in today's world one cannot introduce Christian doctrine out of the blue. A case has to be made for taking it seriously as providing a framework within which a distinctive vision of what human life might be arises and is sustained. So the first three chapters of this collection fall broadly under the heading of natural theology. We need to indicate those features of the human situation which might be held to open up the spiritual dimension, which, of course, is fostered and realised in many different religious traditions. Equally we need to reflect on what difference religion makes to morality, and on how a religious ethic might relate to secular ethics, again in their many different forms. These are the concerns of chapters 1 and 2. I include a slightly more narrowly focused study of Butler on conscience and virtue because Butler's work remains a marvellous example of religious natural law ethics; and the particular scholarly controversy I single out for comment illustrates very well how it is possible to miss this general view of human nature as morally structured in its very essence.

But I am also concerned to bring out the distinctiveness of Christian ethics in a way that does not impose too monolithic and uniform a view of the Christian life. The varieties of goodness discussed in chapter 4 are varieties of Christian goodness, different forms of the moral life that can and should be embraced within the Christian as contrasted with other religious or secular moralities. It is difficult to keep the right balance here between stressing the distinctiveness of the Christian way and allowing for, even encouraging, variety within that distinctive ethical strand. Having stressed the variety in chapter 4, I stress the distinctive framework for that variety in chapters 5 and 6.

But the distinctiveness of Christian ethics can only be understood in relation to and by comparison with the ethical convictions of the other great world faiths. This is the theme around which the six essays forming Part Two of this collection are grouped. Chapter 7 considers the special place of Jewish faith and practice not only for the moral life but also for the Christian doctrine of the Incarnation. If Christian ethics depends on the life, death and resurrection of Jesus Christ, then it depends also on the faith of Israel. For without that tradition and that developing understanding of human life under God, the Incarnation could not have happened. The Christian way, in other words, is essentially bound up with a providential reading of the history of religions.

All this means that I have to take issue with two increasingly popular ways of rethinking the essence of Christianity and of religion. One is the Christian atheism of my friend and colleague, Don Cupitt. The other is the extreme religious pluralism of John Hick. Chapters 8 and 9 are devoted to these issues. If Christian ethics is indeed a theocentric and Christocentric affair, despite its many different guises, it cannot be expressed without genuine dependence on the living God, active and revealed in Christ and the Spirit. This entails belief in the reality of God and a future consummation beyond death. Where these pillars of Christianity (and indeed of most other world faiths) are abandoned, and talk of God and eternity is translated into a purely humanistic faith, the heart of Christianity is gone and the baby poured out with the bathwater. Such a view, of course, puts a big question mark against the adequacy of non-theistic faiths such as early

Buddhism, as indeed the history of religion in India itself suggests.

John Hick's extreme religious pluralism is a more attractive option for those who are convinced of the reality of God and of a 'power not ourselves that makes for righteousness', and yet increasingly appreciative of the faith and spirituality nurtured in the great non-Christian religions of the world. In chapter 9, I take issue with the view that all the great religions are, at least potentially, equally valuable ways of fostering unselfish lives and moral communities centred on God, largely over the question of truth. The extreme pluralist view, I suggest, is false to the distinctive nature, not only of Christianity, but of most other faiths too.

This means that we cannot escape the task of comparative religious ethics and some attempt at cross-cultural evaluation, however difficult this may be to do sensitively and without injustice to the faith of other people. The last three chapters, based on the Teape Lectures given in Delhi, Calcutta and Bangalore in the winter of 1983/4 under the general title, 'The Overcoming of Evil', provide a brief example of how this might be done in relation to one of the most difficult practical as well as theoretical problems facing a religious ethic. I am grateful to the Teape Foundation for inviting me to go to India then and to pursue the topic of comparative religious ethics.

I am grateful, too, to the publishers and editors who have permitted me to reprint those pieces that have already appeared in an earlier form: to the Clarendon Press and Christopher Cunliffe for chapter 3, from *Joseph Butler's Moral and Religious Thought* (1992); to Westminster/John Knox Press and Joseph Runzo for chapter 4, from *Ethics, Religion and the Good Society* (1992); to T. & T. Clark and D. W. Hardy and P. H. Sedgwick for chapter 5, from *The Weight of Glory* (1991); to the *Epworth Review* (September 1992) for chapter 6; to the *Scottish Journal of Theology* (April 1989) for chapter 7; to Macmillan and Joseph Runzo for chapter 8, from *Is God Real?* (1993); and to Macmillan and Arvind Sharma for chapter 9, from *God, Truth and Reality* (1993).

Part One

1

Mystery and humanity[1]

When Paul spoke of himself and his fellow apostles as 'servants of Christ and stewards of the mysteries of God' (1 Cor. 4.1), it was indeed the mysteries of *God* that he had in mind. But it is not unreasonable for the religious apologist today to take the phrase 'stewards of the mysteries' rather more widely and to regard it as his or her task to speak about the mystery of being human, and about those elements in or aspects of humanity that are mysterious and that might be thought to raise the question of God. I take it as axiomatic that apologetics, in our modern godless world, involves entering into and cherishing our common humanity in such a way as to bear witness to those aspects of the human in which the moral and spiritual dimension – and the whole question of God – might come to be discerned. By dwelling on the mysteries of human life we may hope to open up the road to a recovery or discovery of the mysteries of God.

A more technical way of indicating the purpose of this chapter would be to call it an exploration of the rudiments of a religious anthropology from the side of our being human. I want to try to pinpoint what it is about human beings that raises the questions to which religion and particularly Christianity suggest an answer.

However, this method of beginning from below and drawing attention to the mysteries of human life is not just a matter of apologetic strategy. It is a theological necessity in the modern world. Liberal theologians are often criticised by

[1] An earlier version of this chapter was delivered at a Colloquium in Leicester Cathedral in July 1984.

those who want to defend a simple straightforward credal Christianity for bending over backwards to begin from below and to explicate the doctrines of the creed from an anthropological starting point – moreover from a modern, contemporary, anthropological starting point. But in fact this is a theological necessity in a cultural environment which, as has often been pointed out, is deeply and pervasively conditioned by that 'turn to the subject' which characterised not only the thought of the Enlightenment and its aftermath, but also modernity's whole attitude to questions of authority and experience. Of course, there is a danger of reductionism and subjectivism in the attempt to rethink the question of God from this anthropological starting point – and it is true that some theologians have succumbed to this danger. But the vast majority of theologians are endeavouring, not to reduce theology to anthropology, but to help people rediscover the essential religious and Christian truths from the starting point of where they are – culturally and historically as well as individually.[2] This involves much more than the negative method of correlation expounded by Paul Tillich.[3] Tillich first spells out the human existential problems or questions before attempting to show how Christian faith resolves them. But the problems are spelled out in very negative terms. Of course, the negative and problematic side of human life, both personal and social, must be faced and kept in mind throughout this enquiry. But equal stress must be laid on the positive aspects of mystery to be discerned in human life and experience as opening up the dimension of the spirit.

In his book, *Man*,[4] Jürgen Moltmann speaks of the importance for a human being 'to remain conscious of the mystery that he is to other people and that others are to him, and to respect this mystery'. Similarly, in an article on 'Anthropology, Christian',[5] Anthony Dyson writes,

---

[2] See, e.g. David Kelsey's essay, 'Human Being', in P. Hodgson and R. King (eds.), *Christian Theology: an Introduction to its Traditions and Tasks*, London 1983.
[3] P. Tillich, *Systematic Theology*, Vol. I, Welwyn 1953, pp. 67–73.
[4] J. Moltmann, *Man*, London 1974.
[5] A. Dyson, 'Anthropology, Christian', in A. Richardson and J. Bowden (eds.), *A New Dictionary of Christian Theology*, London 1983, pp. 23–6.

It is, all in all, appropriate to describe human existence, in its contradictions and ambiguities, as irreducibly mysterious, as at once dignified and miserable, as human but less than human. To refer to 'mystery' is not to plead for theological silence; it *is* to warn of the dangers of excessive confidence and precision in theological anthropology. Nonetheless the notion of 'mystery' suggests that human life does transcend the temporal system.

There are warnings here about the ambiguities in the human situation and about the limitations to our ability to plumb these mysteries. But the emphasis is on human dignity, and we need to ask, as precisely as the subject-matter permits, what it is about the human that makes such writers use the language of mystery. Dyson speaks of human life *transcending* the temporal system. This is a common starting point in contemporary theology. Karl Rahner wrote of man's self-transcendence,[6] Wolfhart Pannenberg of man's openness to the future.[7] Both theologians take their basic fact of our human freedom to go beyond what the past has furnished us with and create a new future for ourselves and our world as a starting point for Christian anthropological reflection. John Macquarrie, too, links freedom and transcendence, and singles out this human ability to push back the horizons of humanity itself as raising the question of transcendence in the more objective sense of that for which we are reaching out, beyond the limitations of finitude.[8] One notes the way in which such writers refrain from moving straight to the notion of objective, infinite, divine transcendence. They begin with human transcendence, with human beings' reaching out – and only then with the question of what they might be reaching for.

This talk of self-transcendence and openness to the future is pretty abstruse and abstract talk. One has to press the question what precisely it means. But it is worth pausing, even at this very general and abstract level, to reflect on what a remarkable fact it is that a physical universe, consisting of elementary particles, energies and forces, should so evolve,

[6] See, e.g. K. Rahner, *Foundations of Faith*, London 1978, ch. 1.
[7] W. Pannenberg, *What is Man?*, Philadelphia 1970.
[8] J. Macquarrie, *In Search of Humanity*, London 1982.

over time, as to produce not only the conditions of life, not only living beings, but free and rational persons, able to create the future of their world. It was not unreasonable for Teilhard de Chardin, in *The Phenomenon of Man*,[9] to have seen in the emergence, beyond the biosphere, of the noosphere – the world of intelligent thought and free action – not only something quite unique and truly mysterious, but a clue to the meaning and goal of the whole process. The very emergence of persons in cosmic evolution is a great mystery, and a starting point, it may be suggested, for religious reflection. And it is qualities such as freedom, thought, action and creativity that are summed up in phrases such as self-transcendence and openness to the future, and demand reflection on the nature and destiny of a universe capable of producing such things.

We are stressing here the positive features of humanity's self-transcendence, but there is a negative side as well, as Anthony Dyson pointed out, and as we are all very much aware. For this free, creative, self-transcending product of cosmic evolution is a very fragile, ambiguous and incomplete phenomenon. But the negative aspects of human existence are themselves mysterious. Not only do the positive qualities of freedom and creativity point beyond themselves to a possible source and goal of such transcendence, but also our ambiguity and incompleteness and fragility raise the question whether those positive qualities do not somewhere have a surer hold on reality, and a more lasting, unambiguous and perfect source and goal.

The mysterious features, both positive and negative, of being human can be further brought out by reference to the book, *A Rumour of Angels*, by the sociologist, Peter Berger.[10] Berger writes there of 'signals of transcendence', aspects of human experience, which resist the apparently reductive methods of sociological explanation. 'By signals of transcendence', he says, 'I mean phenomena that are to be found within the domain of our "natural" reality but that appear to point beyond that reality.' He singles out such fundamental human traits as human beings' propensity for order, their

[9] P. Teilhard de Chardin, *The Phenomenon of Man*, London 1959.
[10] P. Berger, *A Rumour of Angels*, Baltimore 1969.

fundamental trust in reality as ultimately in order, exemplified even in such simple reassurances as that of the mother to her child: 'everything will be all right'. He also singles out the phenomenon of play, which captures the deathlessness of childhood and in a curious way, like all joy, wills eternity (in Nietzsche's phrase). And then there is the argument from hope – an essential aspect of openness to the future and another instance of fundamental trust in reality. Hope, like play, is indeed a mysterious phenomenon in the face of a godless world. Yet people go on hoping, just as they go on playing. Berger also singles out the phenomenon of moral outrage, the fact that something like the Nazi war crimes cry out not just for disapproval but for absolute condemnation as monstrously evil and a flagrant abuse of the nature of things. Berger also mentions the argument from humour. Humour, like play, is a very mysterious thing. 'The comic', writes Berger, 'reflects the imprisonment of the human spirit in the world.' It is interesting to find a sociologist writing in these terms and drawing attention to what, *qua* sociologist, he cannot explain. And it is significant, for our purposes, that his chapter on the signals of transcendence is entitled 'Starting with Man'.

It might well be thought that moral outrage is the most persuasive of Berger's signals of transcendence. But moral outrage, however striking a fact of life, is a somewhat negative and one-sided aspect of the phenomenon of human existence. We might prefer to focus attention on more positive aspects of our ethical being. This too is a great mystery. 'The moral law within' was one of the two things which moved the philosopher Kant to profound wonder.[11] Part of the task of apologetics is to cultivate this wonder and to resist those tendencies in modern scientific anthropology which reduce humanity to a level below the ethical.

That human beings are appropriate objects of scientific study can hardly be denied. We are products of the evolutionary process. We are made up of stuff which can and should be studied by physicists, chemists and biologists, and our mental and social life is the proper object of study by

---

[11] The other was 'the starry heavens above'.

psychologists, anthropologists and sociologists. But the natural and the human sciences abstract and concentrate on very real and very important aspects of human existence. They attempt to catch the phenomenon of the human, as it were, in a variety of nets, made up of wildly differing meshes; and to a certain extent the nature of the mesh determines what they catch. But none of the sciences can hope to capture the unique individuality of the concrete human being – the person as such, either as an individual or in personal relation to others. Treating persons in relation as persons is, of course, the sphere of ethical concern.

Our initial target here is the rather crude way in which scientific approaches can overstep their limits and attempt a kind of take-over bid on the human. This is what is meant by reductionism. It is the notion that we are nothing but a product of the laws of physics and chemistry, nothing but complex animals, nothing but the result of social or economic laws. An example of such a reductionist approach would be the assimilation of the human mind to a computer and believing that one day we may be able to construct machines endowed with 'artificial intelligence', which will do anything and everything we can do. Another example of reductionism is that of Desmond Morris in his well-known book, *The Naked Ape*,[12] which treats human life entirely in terms of 'behaviour patterns' which we share with the animals, albeit in a more complex way. No doubt such comparisons between animal and human ways of feeding, grooming, sleeping, fighting, mating, and caring for the young, provide illuminating insights into human behaviour, but to imply or assert that they reveal the whole truth about human beings, or even a deeper or more fundamental truth about human existence than is to be found in ethics, philosophy or religion is to go way beyond the actual scientific evidence.

The most serious form of reductionism is that of determinism. The free will versus determinism debate represents the potential clash between science and ethics – and indeed

[12] D. Morris, *The Naked Ape*, London 1967.

between science and religion – at its sharpest. If our actions are not our own, if, that is, what we call our actions are simply the outcome of law-governed prior processes (both external and internal), it would be quite impossible to maintain our ethical concepts or responsibility, and praise and blame. 'Ought' implies 'can'; and free will is integral to our notion of moral personality and to the notion of self-transcendence with which this chapter began. But in fact the thesis of determinism is very far from having been proved; indeed there is a case for thinking that arguments for determinism are self-refuting. The point stressed here is that it is not just religion and ethics but our whole everyday world of thought and action and of interpersonal relation that give the lie to determinism. This is why in practice even the most rigorous scientist will actually treat other human beings as persons, in an ethical perspective, and take part in genuinely ethical debate. If he or she does treat people unethically, this is not *qua* scientist, but as a human being open to ethical rebuke, forgiveness or enlightenment.

In Offenbach's *The Tales of Hoffmann*, the hero, helped by some magic spectacles, falls in love with a clockwork doll. The humour lies in the inappropriate direction of a human emotion such as love to what is in fact an inanimate object, made of cogwheels, springs and wires. It would be equally inappropriate, though not so funny, if he had treated a real woman as if she were made of cogwheels, springs and wires. It would be equally unfunny, equally unethical, if he had treated a real woman as if she were just a household pet or just a sex object. What matters is that a person should be treated appropriately as a person. Now there are some interesting thought experiments to be tried out here. In our actual experience, persons are made of flesh and blood. As far as we know, only highly developed animal organisms can develop the attributes of mind, free will and personality and thus enter the ethical domain. This is a great mystery, why it is that 'soft' matter (protoplasm – the biological organism) has the capacity to develop into persons, while hard matter (silicon chips, electric circuits, etc.) does not. The reason why we dismissed the idea of 'artificial intelligence' just now was that there is no evidence that computers or robots, however 'sophisticated' as we metaphorically say, have the properties of sensation or consciousness, let alone thought or rationality. But of course if it turned out that we were wrong about this, and we did succeed in constructing in the laboratory a robot capable of feeling, consciousness, thought and rationality, we should be morally obliged to treat 'it' ('it' language would become inappropriate, though) as a person, and requiring ethical consideration. The scientists' own creation would then have gone beyond the limits of purely scientific treatment and entered the sphere of the ethical. It would have become mysterious. It is because Olympia in *The Tales of Hoffmann* is not really a person, not even conscious or sentient, that Hoffman's falling in love with 'her' ('her' language in this case being inappropriate) remains comic – though also tragic for Hoffmann.

The kind of reductionism discussed here is relatively crude. It is difficult to carry through consistently into the sphere of action. But it remains a danger, nonetheless. Talk of social engineering or of genetic engineering betrays this tendency towards treating human beings as nothing but objects for manipulation. The inappropriateness of such approaches to the human, if not controlled by ethical considerations, is clear from the metaphor of engineering used in these phrases. This is not to dismiss considerations based on our knowledge of sociology or genetics from social and political planning and decision-making, but it is to insist on their control by ethical considerations, in which the persons involved are always treated as persons – in Kant's terminology, as ends in themselves, never as means only.

There is a rather less crude way in which modern scientific approaches to the study of the human can come to take over or swallow up what we normally think of as the ethical. Consider, for example, the work of sociologists such as E. O. Wilson on apparently ethical notions like altruism.[13] The behaviour of insects, birds and mammals, which appear to sacrifice themselves for the sake of their young or some

[13] See E. O. Wilson, *On Human Nature*, Cambridge, Mass. 1978.

related group, is explained in terms of evolutionary natural selection as furthering the survival of the species, or more plausibly, the gene.[14] In his book, *The Selfish Gene*,[15] Richard Dawkins showed that such 'altruistic' behaviour is a mechanism for preserving and increasing the number of genes of specific kinds rather than for furthering the survival of the species. This is a very interesting hypothesis, and greatly changes our understanding of evolution. At first sight, however, such studies appear to have a very negative effect on ethical concepts such as altruism. It looks as if an ethical concept is being reduced to, or explained away in terms of, a biological mechanism. Once again there appears to be a conflict between scientific and ethical approaches to the study of the human.

But a closer look shows us that this is not necessarily so. Clearly, the terms 'selfish' and 'altruistic', as applied to insects, birds and mammals, let alone to genes, are being used metaphorically. Indeed they are defined by sociobiologists purely behaviouralistically as behaviour furthering the survival or success either of the individual itself, or of the species, or of the gene. Whichever way, it is purely instinctive behaviour. Gulls are not really being selfish in the ethical sense when they drive other gulls away. Ducks are not really being altruistic in the ethical sense when they attract predators to themselves away from their young. In the ethical sense, the terms 'selfish' and 'altruistic' are applied to motives and action for which persons are held responsible and for which they can be praised or blamed. In the ethical sense selfishness and altruism presuppose freedom. No doubt the possibility of altruism in the ethical sense is based on or rooted in the fact of non-ethical behavioural 'altruism'. But the remarkable thing about human beings as persons is that these biological mechanisms are taken over and personalised in the context of freedom and become something quite different from merely instinctive reactions to stimuli. We can no more treat altruism in humans as nothing but a

---

[14] Genes are the sequence of molecules which determine the replication or inheritance of differential characteristics.

[15] R. Dawkins, *The Selfish Gene*, Oxford 1976.

gene-determined behaviour pattern than we can treat thought as determined by patterns of brain activity.

In fact Dawkins is perfectly well aware of this, and *The Selfish Gene* may be regarded as illustrating, not denying, the thesis that ethics transcends science. Dawkins tells us quite explicitly that he is not advocating a morality based on evolution: 'I am saying how things have evolved. I am not saying how we humans ought to behave.'[16] And at the end of the book, he says: 'It is possible that yet another unique quality of man is a capacity for genuine, disinterested, true altruism. I hope so . . .'[17] But, of course, in that case, he should have made it clear that in ascribing 'ruthless selfishness' to our genes he was only speaking metaphorically, and it was thoroughly tendentious of him to scatter the book with remarks like: 'The argument of this book is that we, and all other animals, are machines created by our genes.' The truth is that he does not mean what he says in such throw-away lines. He is not really a reductionist; nor is he really committing the genetic fallacy of thinking that he has fully explained the pheno-menon of altruism by indicating its biological base.

All this goes to show that it is not very difficult to resist scientific reductionism and to defend the mystery of humans as ethical beings. But what of the religious dimension? This comes in when we pause, like Kant, to contemplate, with wonder, the very fact of ethical values in the world. The fact that cosmic evolution can produce ethical beings is one of the springboards of religious faith. Self-transcendence, when con-strued in explicitly ethical terms, is even more a mystery than it is when construed simply in terms of freedom. We may refer again to Berger's point about moral outrage here; for, after all, there are two sides to the ethical. Positive ethical value may itself be a mysterious phenomenon in the world, but so is its precarious and often frustrated nature. It is hard to deny the seriousness and mystery of wickedness. Again we find ourselves asking whether goodness has not somewhere got a surer and more lasting hold on reality than is evidenced by its

[16] Dawkins, *The Selfish Gene*, p. 3.
[17] Dawkins, *The Selfish Gene*, p. 215.

precarious manifestations in the ethical life of humanity. One way of making this point is to say that just as the problem of evil is a great stumbling block for a religious understanding of the world, so the problem of good and its precariousness in the world is a stumbling block for naturalism.

But to return to the positive side – one important aspect of the ethical life, perhaps the most important aspect, is that of interpersonal relation as such. Human capacity for interpersonal relation – for care, affection, friendship and love – are among the most wonderful as well as the most mysterious facets of human existence. And they provide many points at which the religious dimension of existence shines through. This always seems to be at least implicitly recognised in the context of marriage. The capacity of a man and a woman to commit themselves to each other, unreservedly and without qualification, is a remarkable fact about our humanity and cries out for some kind of religious expression. Instinctively we feel that such a deep personal relation speaks to us of eternal things. This sense of the personal as reflecting ultimate reality was given classic expression in Martin Buber's book, *I and Thou*.[18]

Mention of marriage leads one to reflect on the mystery of human sexuality and on how the language of sexual intimacy can become a metaphor for spiritual or mystical union. There are great dangers here and it is clear that human sexuality requires an ethical framework of respect for the other as a person, if the terrible abuses to which the sexual drive is susceptible are to be avoided. But the Christian Church has, for the most part, failed to do justice to the fact of sexual intimacy as a mystery that itself opens up the spiritual dimension.[19]

Ethics is not, of course, only about personal goodness and integrity nor about interpersonal relations and intimacy irrespective of social context. It is also about such things as human rights and social justice – matters which certainly form

---

[18] M. Buber, *I and Thou*, New York 1958.
[19] See the essay, 'Intimacy' by Brian Thorne, reprinted in his *Person-Centred Counselling*, London 1991, ch. 11.

a meeting point for secular and religious concern. Contemporary secular passion for human rights and social justice is indeed an aspect of that modern revolt against authoritarian and hierarchical forms of human community with which Christianity has itself, to its cost, been all too often implicated. But it is not easy to make sense of human rights and social justice as absolute values within a purely secular framework.[20] As Alasdair MacIntyre has pointed out,[21] such values are difficult to defend rationally and soon become no more than matters of political passion and pressure. The absolute value of each person as, to repeat Kant's phrase, an end in himself, is very hard to sustain without a religious, perhaps even a Christian backing, as the history of post-Kantian ethics shows. And it is the absolute value of each person that provides the rational basis for an insistence on human rights and social justice. Not that the religions have been very good themselves at drawing these implications from their frameworks of interpretation, although there are signs that some of them are improving in this respect. The present point, however, is that the social ethical demand for human rights and social justice is a mysterious phenomenon unless accorded a religious basis. Its felt power, therefore, may be regarded as an intimation of that grounding in the ultimate nature of things.

We turn now, briefly, to the mysterious phenomena of art, literature, architecture and music. Stewards of the mysteries should be eager to cherish and foster aesthetic awareness as an aspect of that creativity in self-transcendence which raises the question of God. Here are two examples from the many that could be cited: Bernard Levin on Shakespeare and Karl Barth on Mozart – unexpected sources, since Levin is hardly a religious man and Barth would hardly have approved of his remarks being used for apologetic purposes. First Levin on Shakespeare:

> No other writer has brought us so close to the heart of the ultimate mystery of the universe and of man's place in it. No

---

[20] See ch. 2. below.
[21] A. MacIntyre, *After Virtue*, London 1981.

other has felt and presented the numinous with such certainty and power, no other penetrated so deeply into the source from which he derived his genius and from which we all, including him, derive our humanity. And that is the ultimate pleasure of Shakespeare: the deep sustaining realisation that his work is not only beautiful, thrilling, profound and funny, but, above all, true.[22]

Now Barth on Mozart:

Hearing creation unresentfully and impartially, he did not produce merely music of his own but that of creation . . . He neither needed nor desired to express or represent himself, his vitality, sorrow, piety, or any programme. He was remarkably free from the mania for self-expression. He simply offered himself as the agent by which little bits of horn, metal and catgut could serve as the voices of creation, sometimes leading, sometimes accompanying and sometimes in harmony . . .[23]

These two examples serve to show how the mystery of human creativity in literature and music can open up the religious dimension and speak to us of ultimate things.

But now we turn to the most obvious aspect of the mystery of human existence to which the apologist may appeal, namely the fact that humans, for the most part, have been and are religious beings. This phenomenon is not without its negative side. The history of religions is full of corruptions, perversions and horrors of many kinds. But the fact of mystical experience in every major religious context, the fact of a sense of absolute dependence (stressed by Schleiermacher), and the fact of numinous experience of the holy (stressed by Otto) are all great mysteries, incomprehensible from a secular point of view, which has to explain them away by a variety of more or less implausible theories. The fact is that, even in our own Western secularised, world, there is a great deal of implicit and explicit religious experience – no doubt ill-understood and often open to appalling distortion and abuse, but nevertheless constituting a vast field of phenomena with which

---

[22] *The Listener*, 26 August 1982.
[23] K. Barth, *Church Dogmatics*, III/3, Edinburgh 1960, pp. 297ff. See now, also, H. Küng, *Mozart. Traces of Transcendence*, London 1992.

to make contact when offering religious interpretations of the world.

We have tried so far to stress the positive mysteries of human existence which might be held to point to the spiritual dimension, even in our modern, Western, secularised, cultural environment. But throughout we have had to touch on the negative side as well – the precariousness or value, the prevalence of wickedness, the susceptibility of even the best elements in human life and experience to distortion, perversion and abuse. But we have not allowed the negative side to obscure the positive elements of mystery. As Austin Farrer puts it, 'Corruption is a real and terrible thing, but it is distributed partially over man's whole moral nature, and is not the extinction of any particular elements in it.'[24] But it is hard to deny that the experience of evil, of wickedness and suffering, of the precariousness of the good in the world as we experience it, can themselves be felt as mysteries requiring explanation such as Christianity gives in its doctrines of sin and redemption. However, the dark side of human life need not always be our starting point.

Among the negative aspects of human being is, of course, the fact of our mortality. Death is a great mystery, just as life is. But the death of a human being, though inevitable, especially the death of someone we know and love, is one of the most perplexing phenomena in our experience, and the more so the more we have come to appreciate the positive mysteries of creativity, morality, personal relation, beauty and spirituality. It is our mortality more than anything else that underlines the precariousness of those values, and makes us wonder whether goodness and beauty and love do not have a more secure and permanent home. Human hope, despite mortality, was one of Berger's signals of transcendence. And it is part of that fundamental trust in reality of which Hans Küng makes so much in his great apologetic work, *Does God Exist?*[25] One of the few weaknesses of John Macquarrie's *In Search of*

[24] A. M. Farrer, 'The Christian Doctrine of Man', in *Interpretation and Belief*, London 1976. pp. 69–94.
[25] H. Küng, *Does God Exist?*, London 1980.

Humanity[26] (as of his earlier *Christian Hope*)[27] is that his idea of creation culminating in the divine memory prevents him from making very much of our intimations of immortality. Admittedly belief in life after death is more likely nowadays in the West to be an implication of robust and confident faith in God than of anthropological reflection. To that extent our modern secular anthropology has prevailed. Nevertheless experience of the mystery of the death of persons can still prompt the religious sense that death is not the end.

In conclusion, we will introduce some Christological points into our reflections on the mysteries of life. One cannot move directly from such anthropological reflections as have been offered in this chapter straight into Chalcedonian orthodoxy. At most these reflections on the mysteries of human life may open up the moral and spiritual dimensions and suggest intimations of a mind and heart of love at the origin and in the depths of things. But the nature of that transcendent source and goal of all there is very imperfectly intuited from such reflections. Christian theologians cannot deduce the doctrines of the Trinity and Incarnation from these anthropological insights. But if we shift attention to the remarkable historical figure of Jesus of Nazareth and to the historical tradition of faith created by his life and death and their aftermath, we discover new material, not only revelatory of God, but also enhancing the mystery of the human. This goes both for the origins of Christology – that man, his life, his teaching, his passion and death and what came after are all full of mystery – and also it goes for the developed faith of the Christian Church. For if God, in the Person of his Son, became incarnate in and as a particular human being at a particular place and time, that says something quite astonishing about the nature of the human as *capax infiniti*. The mystery of humanity is infinitely enhanced if a particular woman can become the mother of God and a particular man can be the Word Incarnate. The great mystery of the Incarnation, then, not only reveals the mystery of God. It reinforces, beyond

[26] See note 9.
[27] J. Macquarrie, *Christian Hope*, London 1978.

measure, the mystery of humanity. But this, of course, is part of what the Christian faith brings to rather than finds in anthropological reflection.

2

Can moral beliefs be true or false?

It is an interesting fact of cultural history that philosophical ideas, at first known and discussed by only a small minority of intellectuals in the literary world or in the world of higher education, gradually come to percolate through to the populace at large through the education system and the media, first, I suppose, to the more articulate part of the reading public, then to the semi-educated, and then to the majority of our fellow-citizens. The result is that popular attitudes often reflect, in a pretty watered down way, philosophical views first put forward decades or even a century or two ago.

One example of this is the view that science and religion are incompatible, another the widespread belief that one encounters today, especially among young people, that moral beliefs are not true or false. Many people think that moral beliefs are quite unlike factual beliefs, say, about the number of moons Jupiter has or the chemical composition of water. Factual beliefs, people think, concern matters that exist or obtain quite independently of any of us. Jupiter has the number of moons it has whatever any of us are doing or thinking, and would continue to do so even if there were no people left to hold beliefs about how many moons it has, whereas moral beliefs are inextricably bound up with people's feelings and preferences. If you think it wrong to rob the rich to help the poor – I deliberately choose an example of a belief that some people would not agree with – well, that is an expression of your attitude. You *disapprove* of robbing the rich to help the poor. Of course, there is a big question about whether moral beliefs express individual approvals and disapprovals, or whether they express society's approvals and disapprovals. But either way, they are not true or false. They are attitudes or values which we (or society) choose or commend and, certainly, encourage others to choose or commend. But people (and societies) make different choices where morality is concerned. They hold different values systems and commend different ideals. After all, some people (and groups) think it *right* to rob the rich to help the poor.

This widely held view that moral beliefs are quite different from factual beliefs and cannot be thought of as true or false like factual beliefs can be, goes back in modern Western culture at least to the philosophy of David Hume in the eighteenth century and is known as the fact/value distinction.[1] It has percolated down to the populace at large in the way I described and has become a kind of basic assumption in the minds of very many people today.

The concomitant view of moral beliefs or value judgements as expressions of our approvals or disapprovals (and not factual beliefs that might be true or false) is known as 'emotivism'. In saying something is good or bad, right or wrong, we are expressing our feelings about the matter in question. Crudely this has been called the 'boo–hurrah' theory of morals. When I call some deed or person wicked, I am saying 'boo' to it or to him or her. When I call some deed or person good, I am saying hurrah to it or to him or her. Now admittedly, as already pointed out, one can be more or less individualistic about this. At the most individualistic or subjectivist end of the spectrum, as in some forms of existentialism, it is my personal attitudes of approval or disapproval that I am expressing in using moral language. My approvals may be similar to yours, they may partly overlap, or they may be quite different. A much less individualistic view is that our society develops a set of values, things it approves and disapproves, and parents and schools and public opinion attempt to train us to say boo or hurrah to the things it says boo or hurrah to. But, of course, there is no guarantee that

---

[1] See W. D. Hudson (ed.), *The Is–Ought Question*, London 1969.

such training or indoctrination will be successful. It is only too easy for people to rebel against society's views or their parents' views. We may notice that other societies, in other parts of the world, or at different times in history, say boo or hurrah to different things, and we may find ourselves approving or disapproving rather differently from the way in which we were brought up to approve or disapprove. Our society may disapprove of sex before marriage, for example, and have tried to teach us to say boo to it. But perhaps we find ourselves wanting to say hurrah to it. Or things might be the other way round. Maybe we are the children of parents from the permissive sixties reacting against that generation. They said hurrah to sex before marriage, but we have come round to saying boo to it.

It is very difficult to see how, on this emotivist or 'boo–hurrah' theory, moral disputes could ever be resolved. People just do have different values. Of course, they argue about right and wrong. They draw attention to these facts or those facts. And obviously if people are wrong about the facts and hold false factual beliefs, then there is some scope for shifting their attitudes. But if facts and values are in the end of the day absolutely distinct in the way emotivist theory says they are, then arguments about facts are not going to settle fundamental moral disputes. All we are actually doing is producing rationalisations of moral views we cling to emotively. The result is that people with different values tend to resort to persuasive techniques to try to get their way. They form pressure groups and hold demonstrations and make a nuisance of themselves in order to get the authorities to give in or at least compromise.

This whole state of affairs has been very well described in one of the best and most widely discussed books of moral philosophy to have appeared in recent decades – Alasdair MacIntyre's *After Virtue*.[2] MacIntyre shows very clearly how the vocabulary of moral reason and argument has broken down in the wake of this emotivist theory of ethics.

But people are not always consistent over such matters. Those who say that they are emotivists in ethics – people who

---

[2] A. MacIntyre, *After Virtue*, London 1981.

hold to the view that moral beliefs are expressions of approval and disapproval and that values are our own attitudes and ideals – very often behave and talk as if their own moral beliefs were, after all, *true*. Let us take an example. Suppose you feel very strongly about the wrongness of racial discrimination. You go on demonstrations against it. You support civil rights movements. You rejoice at the ending of apartheid in South Africa. But are you really satisfied with the analysis of the statement, 'Racial discrimination is wrong', as meaning 'I (or we) strongly disapprove of racial discrimination'? Is there not a sense in which you want to say that the statement, 'Racial discrimination is wrong', is a *true* statement. It states a fact. It cannot be exhaustively analysed in terms of my (or our) feelings of disapprobation. Saying that it is wrong does not just mean saying boo to it. We say boo to it, rather, because we believe, deeply, that it is wrong.

Admittedly there are right-wing Boers in the Transvaal who feel equally strongly that apartheid was right, who express approval of it and say hurrah to it. But do we not think that they are mistaken? It is not just that we disapprove of their attitudes. We think that what they believe – namely that apartheid was a good thing – is just *false*.

Some years ago there was an editorial in the magazine, *India Today*,[3] which referred to the sad contrast between Mahatma Gandhi's movement of non-violent civil disobedience against British colonialism in India in the earlier half of this century and the tendency in India today for any protesting group to resort to strikes and civil disobedience at the slightest pretext, however unreasonable, even when the democratic process is there and available to channel and resolve disagreements. Gandhi called his movement '*satyagraha*' – truth-force. The force behind his civil disobedience was the truth that colonialism was wrong. The present situation, by contrast, so said that editorial, is nothing but *satyagraha* without *satya* – truth-force without truth – in other words, just force. Here is yet more evidence, from quite another tradition, to indicate the desirability of our being able to appeal to moral truth.

[3] An admirable magazine, very informative about all aspects of life in the Indian sub-continent.

What we are saying when we say that statements like, 'racial discrimination is wrong' and 'colonialism is wrong' express moral truths and not just attitudes is that their wrongness is a fact, whatever people think or feel about them, just as the number of Jupiter's moons is what it is whatever people think about them. The wrongness of apartheid does not depend on people's attitudes nor does it consist in people's attitudes. The boo–hurrah theory simply cannot be right.

But the emotivist may well come back at us like this: I admit, he may say, that moral beliefs have the appearance of objectivity. It looks as if a statement like, 'racial discrimination is wrong' is a true statement, stating a fact. But that is because we have built the notion of objectivity and factuality into our moral language. We bring children up to think of right and wrong as something objective in the nature of things, and the way we talk in moral discourse reflects this. It is a device to reinforce society's values, and to make it more difficult for people to rebel and embrace different values. The emotivist may even agree that society works better like that, and that people in general flourish better when they treat values as if they were objective. But, he will go on, things cannot really be like that. Facts and values *are* distinct. The wrongness of racial discrimination is not really part of the furniture of the world like the number of Jupiter's moons or the chemical composition of water. As David Hume said long ago,[4] when I actually examine a case of wilful murder, all I can objectively discern is X shooting Y dead, X's motive – the desire to avenge an injury or whatever – and what we all feel about the deed – disapproval, no doubt. When I examined apartheid in South Africa, all I objectively discerned was white discrimination against blacks, especially over political rights, and the strong feelings of disapproval which this elicited in the majority of people everywhere, though not in the Boers of the Transvaal, of course. Objectively, the emotivist insists, the wrongness of racial discrimination cannot be demonstrated. For there are no objective values in the sense in which there are objective empirical facts like the number of Jupiter's moons.

[4] D. Hume, *A Treatise of Human Nature*, Book III, Part I, Section I

It should be pointed out that one unfortunate consequence of the view that the apparent objectivity of values is a social device designed to reinforce their hold on us is that the device will only work so long as we do not realise that it is a device. For if we come to appreciate the fact that moral language is only invested with 'truth-force' in order to sustain and encourage socially sanctioned approvals and disapprovals, it will inevitably lose that force and social values will the more easily be overthrown. So society has an interest in concealing the fact that there are no objective values. People will flourish better in society if, as with Plato's 'noble lie',[5] they are deceived into thinking the moral beliefs they are indoctrinated with in infancy to be true beliefs.

So we are back with the state of affairs portrayed by MacIntyre. Modern moral philosophy has undermined the fictions that in the past held society together, and the result is a free-for-all of competing pressure groups and life-styles – the only thing preventing complete chaos being the happy fact that most of us do as a matter of empirical fact like fairness and dislike discrimination.

We cannot leave the matter there. Let us come back to the question of moral truths and explore more carefully what might be meant by talk of moral beliefs as being true or false and what grounds we might have for thinking that there are, after all, moral truths stating moral facts.

We shall eventually be examining and defending a theological ethic as the best way of understanding and accounting for the objectivity of moral value. But before that task is undertaken, let us stay with secular ethics and see whether there is not, after all, some way of defending the notion of moral truth without bringing religion or God into it. One might well imagine secular moralists themselves to be dissatisfied with the situation in modern moral philosophy depicted here, namely, an insistence on the fact/value distinction, a denial of the objectivity of value, and an analysis of

---

[5] Plato, *Republic* 414d. The Guardians in Plato's ideal state are permitted to deceive the populace for their own good. See K. R. Popper, *The Open Society and its Enemies*, London 1945, esp. vol. I, p. 270.

moral language in emotivist terms, with only the appearance of objectivity built into the language in order to reinforce society's approvals and disapprovals – a situation which, once recognised as being so, leads to the abandonment, not only of moral consensus but of moral reasoning, and the consequent resort to persuasive techniques, pressure groups, and manipulation, as rival factions try to get their own way. How might a secular moralist attempt to resist this rather depressing picture?

It is not entirely clear that he can resist this. But let us at least try to construct a purely secular, humanist, way of rescuing the objectivity of value. To do so, we would have to go right back to square one and question the fact/value distinction. Why should we operate with such a limited sense of fact as the fact/value distinction requires? Certainly the fact that Jupiter has twelve moons is a fact quite independent of anything about us. But there are many facts about us as well. Emotivists themselves are always talking about our feelings of approval and disapproval. They are facts too, like all our thoughts and purposes and desires and beliefs and sensations. Moreover, not all the facts involving us are private and subjective like those mental states and acts undoubtedly are. The greenness of grass is an objective fact about grass, but it depends on people like ourselves observing the grass. For colours are how things of certain pigmentation look to beings sensitive to the colour spectrum in the way we are. The greenness of grass is an interesting example of an objective fact that nevertheless depends on our being here and being the sort of beings we are. What about the wrongness of racial discrimination? Certainly, if that is a fact, it is not like the number of Jupiter's moons – something that obtains entirely irrespective of our being here. But is the wrongness of racial discrimination like the green colour of grass or is it like my preference for blondes? Surely, the humanist could argue that it is more like the green colour of grass, in that it depends not on *my* mental states but on human beings in general being what they are. In the nature of things, human beings in general have similar potentialities and needs. Each counts for one; yet each needs other people in society if his or her potentialities are to be realised and his or her needs met. No man is an island. So it follows from the basic facts of human nature and needs that the claims of other people press upon us with objective force. Our convictions about human rights are, like our sense of fairness, grounded in what it is to be a human being. It is entirely natural and intelligible that children in a family should not only want to be treated fairly but feel very strongly that it is wrong if one of them is singled out for preferential treatment and the others ignored. Note that we think this not just where *we* have been unfairly treated, but when any child in any family is being unfairly treated. Similarly in games, the very nature and point of the game makes it wrong for the umpire to favour one side rather than the other. So, our secular humanist might argue, in the great game of life, human rights are objectively grounded in what it is to be a human being in relation to other human beings. The wrongness of racial discrimination is like the wrongness of unfair play or unfair treatment of a child at home or at school. It is not just based on people's preferences. On the contrary, one's disapproval reflects the very nature of humanity and the conditions that, quite objectively, make for human flourishing. The sense of racial discrimination being objectively wrong is not a social device designed to give our disapproval of it the feel of objectivity. It is based on the facts about humanity and is therefore itself a human or moral fact. Consequently the possibility of moral reasoning comes back after all. We do not have immediately to resort to pressure groups for change. We reason with our opponents, appealing to the facts of human nature and needs and the conditions that can be shown to make for human flourishing or to inhibit it.

Well, we have done our best on the secular humanist's behalf. But does this view of the matter really work? Have we really succeeded in establishing the objectivity of value and demonstrating that moral facts are there to be discerned among the furniture of the world?

It is sad to have to answer, no. One would gladly welcome a view of human nature that presented us objectively with moral claims. But many people will probably remain unconvinced that moral *obligation* is rooted in the nature of things. After all, all our secular humanist has said is that the statement, 'Racial discrimination is wrong' is not just an expression of *my* dislike of racial discrimination; rather, racial discrimination can be shown to be inconsistent with the nature and needs of people in general and with the conditions that make for human flourishing. One can call that a moral truth if one likes, but we have still not succeeded in bringing out the *obligation* to oppose racial discrimination. The emotivist can always come back in and say that our opposition to what contradicts the conditions of human flourishing is still a matter of feeling.

Consider the child's sense of fair play once again. It is a moral truth, in a sense, that preferential treatment among siblings is unfair. But my sense of unfair treatment is a matter of feeling. And if I feel equally bad about you being unfairly treated, that too depends on a fellow feeling which, even among siblings, cannot be guaranteed, as parents know only too well.

The emotivist can always say that our commitment to human rights in general as alone respecting the facts of human nature and needs rests on nothing but a strong fellow-feeling – sympathy for our fellow human beings. But can that by itself support the weight of obligation? It seems not. The Boers in the Transvaal believe that *they* are unlikely to flourish better now that the blacks in South Africa have the vote, and their *interest* most likely outweighs any general humanitarian feeling they may in theory have acquired or been taught. And they may turn on us and say that we can afford to indulge our humanitarian feelings on the blacks' behalf, since our interests are not threatened.

It looks as if emotivism triumphs again, even when we recognise certain moral truths bound up with the nature and needs of humanity as such. For at best they yield what the philosopher, Kant, called hypothetical imperatives.[6] If you want humanity in general to flourish, then you should indeed oppose racial discrimination; for it is certainly true that racial

[6] I. Kant, *Groundwork of the Metaphysic of Morals*, ch. 2.

discrimination contradicts the nature and needs of humanity in general. But of what Kant called categorical imperatives – you ought to oppose racial discrimination come what may – ethical naturalism, the view that human nature determines moral truths, gives no account at all.

Let us, then, go right over to the other end of the spectrum of moral theories and set out a view which does establish moral truths of an absolutely categorical nature, a view that has no 'ifs' about it, but asserts, and indeed explains, the *fact* that we human beings stand inexorably under certain basic moral obligations, whether we like it or not. I am referring, of course, to theological ethics, the view that it is God's nature and will that determine moral truths and their claim on us.

We should begin by pointing out that theological ethics involves from the start a complete denial of the fact/value distinction. For the ultimate fact – the reality of God as Creator of the world – is itself supremely valuable. God is in essence perfectly good, necessarily so. Being God and being necessarily good are one and the same thing. Christianity spells this out with its understanding of God as Love. God *is* Love. There is no way in which you can prize fact and value apart where God is concerned. This means that God is not only the source of all being other than himself; he is at the same time the source of all value. This is reflected in the creation. 'God saw what he had made and behold it was very good' (Gen. 1.31). In other words, the world as creation has a derived *value*. It is not just here in a neutral way, distinct from any value. It has a value, a meaning, and a goal, in the Creator's intention. Admittedly, we can investigate the world in a value–neutral way, as we do in science, or when we are counting Jupiter's moons, but that is to abstract from the full reality of the world whose ultimate goodness and beauty reflect the Creator's nature and will. Nowhere is this more so, according to Christian theology, than in the case of human beings, made in the image of God. Human beings have the value that they have – each as an end in himself or herself and never to be used only as a means[7] – just because each is a child of God,

[7] Kant, loc. cit.

destined for eternity; and human beings stand under a categorical obligation to respect each other's rights, and indeed to love their neighbour (and all people are potentially my neighbours) just because they are intended by their Creator to reflect and correspond to his own perfect nature as love.

Earlier in this chapter we considered the attempt by secular moralists dissatisfied with emotivism as an account of value, to ground both value and obligation in the nature and needs of humanity. That was not an easy task for people who think that human beings are, ultimately speaking, nothing but the products of random combinations of material substance over cosmic evolution. The theological ethicist is much better placed to ground both value and obligation in the nature and needs of humanity because, for a religion like Christianity, the fundamental truth about human beings is that they are God's children, destined to be finite images of the divine love. That is the fundamental *truth* about humans; and moral beliefs are true or false in so far as they correspond or fail to correspond to these fundamental facts.

Clearly a theological ethic makes much better sense of human rights and the obligation to respect and further human rights than does any other theory. We oppose racial discrimination not just because we do not like it, nor just because it contradicts some conception of human flourishing to which we feel committed, but because it flagrantly flouts the Creator's intention and will – namely that all men and women should respect and love each other as God himself loves us. The belief that racial discrimination is wrong is a true belief because it corresponds to these ultimate facts concerning the nature and destiny of man or woman as the image and child of God who is Love.

There are, of course, a number of problems with such a heavily theological ethic. Are we not tying moral facts – the wrongness of racial discrimination, for example – much too closely to a set of highly specific theological truth claims about God, creation and human destiny, which can hardly be taken for granted as true? Indeed, considered impartially, these immense truth claims about God, creation and human destiny are far less certain than the wrongness of racial discrimination. Even worse, does not my theological explanation of moral facts render secular ethics quite incomprehensible? How can there be morality without religion on this view? And yet far more people than religious believers are convinced of the wrongness of racial discrimination and committed to the struggle for human rights. Recall the hoary old problem for theological ethics summed up under the heading of the Euthyphro dilemma,[8] namely, the dilemma as to whether something is good because God commands it or whether God commands it because it is good. The first horn looks highly dubious since anything God commanded – say, torture – would on that score be good by definition. The second horn looks equally dubious from the theological ethical point of view, since, if God commands something because it is good, then it is good already, so why bring God into it?

The dilemma is easily resolved. We did not in any case set out a theological ethic in terms of divine commands. We spoke of God's will reflecting God's nature as absolute perfection. There is no question of God commanding torture. All God's commands are bound to reflect his essential goodness. But the second horn of the dilemma is quite acceptable too. For, if God commands something because it is good, that does not mean that it is good quite independently of God. Human goodness, for example, already reflects God's will in creation and hence his supreme goodness as source of all value in creation.

But this solution to the Euthyphro dilemma already shows how we can solve the problem – for a theological ethic – of morality without religion. For if God has built value into his creation so that human goodness in itself reflects his nature and will – people do not have to know this fundamental fact about the origin and basis of goodness to be able to recognise it when they see it. In reality, we may say, from a theological ethical point of view, human goodness – human love, human care for the weak, human commitment to human rights – all these things reflect God's will in creation. But we do not have

---

[8] Named after Plato's dialogue, *Euthyphro*, where it was first raised.

to know this in order to feel the claims of these virtues on our moral nature.

So our first problem is resolved as well. It should not surprise us that more people are convinced of the claims of human rights than are convinced of their grounding in the nature and will of the Creator. What we see in humanity itself is, of course, more immediate and accessible than what we see of God as he is in himself. If God has written moral truths into creation, then more men and women are likely to stumble across them there than are likely to achieve the insights of religious faith.

But not all our problems are so happily resolved. For we are left with the difficulty that has been with us throughout this chapter, namely the mysterious nature of moral truths as grasped by purely human insight. Mercifully, commitment to human rights, and conviction, say, of the wrongness of racial discrimination are increasingly widespread phenomena. But how do we account for these things? Rational, secular, minds are vulnerable to emotivism and its conviction of the subjectivity of value. Only a theological ethic can give an account of the moral truths that continue to impress themselves upon us.

3

Butler on conscience and virtue

'Butler exalts conscience, but appears ignorant that a man's conscience may tell him to do the vilest things.' So writes Elizabeth Anscombe in a much discussed paper on 'Modern Moral Philosophy'.[1] This scathing observation about Butler's ethical theory is intended to support a case for locating authority in morals in the divine law over against us rather than in some principle of our own human nature. It is part of Anscombe's argument for holding that without a religious foundation morality loses its obligatory claim and, indeed, should be replaced by sociology. Sociologists, the implication is, are well aware how fallible the psychologically and socially reinforced human mechanism of conscience is. It is a dangerous illusion to exalt conscience. From a religious perspective, it is to put something human and fallible in the place of the divine law. From a non-religious perspective, it is to risk exalting prejudice or some ideologically blinkered judgement or reaction.

In a paper published in the *Journal of the History of Philosophy*,[2] B. Szabados replies to Anscombe's charge by claiming that, had Anscombe considered Butler's Sermons VII, 'Upon the Character of Balaam' and X, 'Upon Self-Deceit', instead of concentrating on Sermons I–III, 'Upon Human Nature', she would have realised that Butler himself was perfectly well aware how self-deceit can corrupt

---

[1] G. E. M. Anscombe, 'Modern Moral Philosophy', reprinted in *Ethics, Politics and Religion*, Collected Papers Vol. 3, Oxford 1981, p. 27.
[2] B. Szabados, 'Butler on Currupt Conscience', *Journal of the History of Philosophy*, vol. 14, 1976, pp. 462–9.

conscience. Butler's system is quite capable of recognising and accounting for the fact that conscience may tell a man to do the vilest things. A corrupt conscience is quite possible. What Butler exalts is a conscience free from such corruption. But there is no need to look outside human nature for authority in morals. Equipped with an error theory, such as Butler's psychologically acute understanding of self-deceit, the moralist can avoid the pitfalls unfairly attributed to Butler by Anscombe and retain a naturalistic ethic in which an uncorrupted conscience plays the leading role.

The study of Butler on conscience and virtue that follows is intended to show that neither Anscombe nor Szabados is right. In no way could Butler possibly concede that *conscience* may tell a man to do the vilest things. But Butler's exaltation of conscience is not part of a humanist or purely naturalistic ethic. Butler's ethic, it will be argued, has an essential religious foundation. It is not a divine command theory, but it *is* a form of religious natural law theory, with conscience possessing its supreme authority solely because that is how the Author of nature intended things to be.

Butler certainly exalts conscience. Over and above our various particular passions and our basic long-term principles of benevolence and self-love, 'there is a superior principle of reflection or conscience in every man, which . . . passes judgement upon himself . . .'.[3] Butler is not saying simply that we find ourselves approving of some of our actions and disapproving of others, as David Hume was soon to say. For Butler, dictates of conscience have an inherent and supreme *authority*. 'Conscience or reflection . . . plainly bears upon it marks of authority over all the rest [namely, the other passions and principles of human nature] and claims the absolute direction of them all . . .'[4] This superiority and direction is 'a constituent part of the idea [namely, of conscience] . . . and to preside and govern, from the very economy and constitution of man, belongs to it.'[5] He goes on, in the same paragraph, to insist that this does not mean that conscience is the most

[3] J. Butler, *Fifteen Sermons Preached at the Rolls Chapel*, Sermon II, para. 8.
[4] Butler, Preface to *Fifteen Sermons*.
[5] Butler, Sermon II, para. 14.

powerful principle in man. It is a question of right, not of power. 'Had it strength, as it has right; had it power, as it has manifest authority, it would absolutely govern the world.' But the implication is that conscience does not have such power. Men act against their conscience; but their conscience authoritatively condemns them when they do so, as even Richard III's did at the end of Shakespeare's play.

For Butler, a virtuous life consists in a hierarchically ordered system of propensities and principles, with benevolence (and cool self-love) controlling passion and interest, and with conscience ruling over all. There is a very interesting passage towards the end of 'A Dissertation upon the Nature of Virtue' in which Butler rejects as a 'terrible mistake' the notion that virtue is to be *equated* with benevolence, with acquisition, that is, of a settled disposition always to promote the happiness of others. Certainly we find in the Sermons such remarks as this: 'it is manifest that the common virtues, and the common vices of mankind, may be traced up to benevolence or the want of it.'[6] But, in man, benevolence cannot be allowed to override conscience. Our duty is to try to promote the happiness of others 'within the bounds of veracity and justice'. For conscience condemns lying, violence and injustice, irrespective of any beneficial consequences that such things might have. We get here a categorical rejection of utilitarianism before that theory was explicitly advanced. Butler allows that God may be a utilitarian, but we human beings lack the omniscience which that theory requires if it is to have any plausibility at all: '. . . were the Author of Nature to propose nothing to himself as an end but the production of happiness, were his moral character merely that of benevolence; yet ours is not so.'[7] Our moral character, our human virtue, is rather a matter of benevolence within the framework of conscience. Conscience, not benevolence, has the last word.

It will already be apparent from this account of conscience and its relation to virtue in Butler's thought how impossible it

---

[6] Butler, Sermon XII, para. 31.
[7] J. Butler, *A Dissertation on the Nature of Virtue*, para. 8.

would have been for Butler to concede to Anscombe that 'a man's conscience may tell him to do the vilest things'. Two further aspects of Butler's view of conscience may be cited in support of this contention. In the first place, conscience is clearly, for Butler, a faculty of *true* discrimination. This is not simply a matter of moral sentiment. Conscience does include felt reaction, but primarily it is a matter of reflection and sovereign judgement, both negative and positive. Conscience convicts a person of wrong motive or action; and it presses the claim of the good. All that Butler says about its authority and its right militates against the possibility of error here.

A mark of this infallibility is the uniformity of conscience. Butler holds that conscience delivers the same judgements the world over. To quote again from the Dissertation:

> 'Nor is it at all doubtful in the general what course of action this faculty . . . approves and what it disapproves. For, as much as it has been disputed wherein virtue consists, or whatever ground for doubt there may be about particulars; yet, in general, there is in reality a universally acknowledged standard of it. It is that which all ages and all countries have made profession of in public; it is that which . . . the primary and fundamental law of civil constitutions over the face of the earth make it their business and endeavour to enforce the practice of upon mankind: namely, justice, veracity and regard to common good.'[8]

So how can Szabados defend Butler against Anscombe by appealing to the former's recognition of the possibility of a corrupt conscience? Careful study of Sermons VII and X will show that Szabados has misinterpreted Butler here. These two sermons are indeed remarkable case studies, the first of Balaam in the book of Numbers, the second of King David in 2 Samuel, chapter 12 – the Bathsheba episode. With the most acute psychological penetration, Butler shows how in each of these cases self-deceit makes a good man suppress conscience and, for a time, acquiesce in wickedness with a quiet mind. Now it is perfectly true, as Szabados points out, that, at the end of Sermon X, Butler speaks of self-deceit as 'this deep and calm source of delusion; which undermines the whole

---

[8] Butler, *Dissertation*, para. 1.

principle of good; darkens that light, that candle of the Lord within, which is to direct our steps; and corrupts conscience, which is the guide of life'.[9] It is this passage that gives Szabados the title of his article: 'Butler on Corrupt Conscience'. But, despite Butler's own reference to self-deceit corrupting conscience, his system *cannot* seriously allow that conscience as such becomes corrupt and, in Anscombe's words, tells a man to do the vilest things. That Butler's rhetoric is, for once, loose and exaggerated here, is shown by his mention in this very passage of notions like 'that candle of the Lord', and 'the guide of life'. These could never be characterised as corrupt in themselves. King David may have been corrupted by self-deceit, but his *conscience* was only buried or suppressed till Nathan roused it with his famous parable. It was not David's *conscience* that told him to steal another man's wife and send her husband to inevitable death at the front. It was desire, buttressed by rationalisation and self-deceit. Similarly in Shakespeare's play, King Richard's conscience was belatedly awoken on the eve of Bosworth Field. It was not his conscience that had previously prompted his string of murders.

Butler writes more accurately and strictly in the course of his other study, Sermon VII, 'Upon the Character of Balaam'. There he speaks of 'half-deceit', 'equivocation', 'subterfuges' as infecting Balaam's character; and then adds: 'By these means, conscience may be laid asleep, and [men] may go on in a course of wickedness with less disturbance.'[10] The key idea, for Butler, in both these sermons, is the possibility, not of a corrupted conscience that itself becomes a source of wickedness, but a conscience put to sleep or suppressed, so that wickedness may have free rein. There is always the hope and possibility that it can be roused from sleep, as David's was by Nathan and Balaam's by his ass. Not only is this so with fundamentally good characters, temporally self-deceived as in Butler's two examples, but also with wicked and depraved characters, like Shakespeare's Richard. Or, to take another example, this time from Peter Geach: if a dedicated Nazi

---

[9] Butler, Sermon X, para. 16.
[10] Butler, Sermon VII, para. 10.

gunner, wounded and bleeding to death, stays at his post, machine-gunning a column of refugees rather than seeking medical help,[11] it may be a perverted *sense* of duty that dictates this action, but it would not on Butler's view be the man's conscience that told him to go on shooting. The Nazi's conscience would have been put pretty thoroughly to sleep by indoctrination in a wicked ideology. But there would always have been the possibility, however remote or faint, of its re-awakening – say, through his suddenly seeing a childhood friend among the column of refugees – and of the gunner coming to himself, realising what he was doing, and repenting in dust and ashes. Conscience as such, then, for Butler, retains its infallibility and authority, even if suppressed and put to sleep. There is always the possibility of its awakening.

But, if we cannot defend Butler against Anscombe along Szabados' path of making Butler concede the point, surely the most plausible move is simply to agree with Anscombe against Butler and say that Butler was quite wrong to exalt conscience as universal, infallible and supremely authoritative in human nature. Our post-Freudian and sociologically aware generation is bound to be highly suspicious, not only of what Butler says about the uniformity and infallibility of conscience, but also about its intrinsic authority. We may be prepared to respect people's conscientious decisions – out of a deeper respect for their rights as autonomous moral agents – but we will often think them wrong for all that. And there are limits to such respect. We do not allow a Jehovah's Witness or a Christian Scientist parent to veto a blood transfusion for an injured child. More broadly, we are all aware of differences of moral judgement amongst the different peoples and cultures of the world, past and present. We will be liable to think of conscience as a product of education and peer group pressure, a process continued in general social conditioning throughout our adult lives. We are familiar with Freud's account of conscience:[12] our primitive drives get repressed

---

[11] P. T. Geach, 'The Moral Law and the Law of God', in *God and the Soul*, London 1969, p. 122.

[12] See, e.g. S. Freud, *Civilisation and its Discontents* (1930).

under parental and social disapproval and this disapproval gets internalised as what Freud calls the 'superego', a kind of internal censor of socially unacceptable desires and deeds. Admittedly Freud's own account concentrates on and appears most plausible in respect of the negative phenomena of guilt. But a similar sociological account of positive moral discrimination can quite easily be given, as it is by secular ethicists such as J. L. Mackie:[13] our positive moral judgements, expressing that which claims and inspires our commitments and allegiances, are also the product of training and socialisation and social interaction.

However, there are certain basic features of the moral life to which these naturalistic, psychological or sociological, accounts fail to do justice. They fail to bring out or account for the *overriding* claims of morality. They fail to explain the way in which our conscience sometimes leads us to stand out against the crowd, against the mores of society. They fail to capture the way in which even a man like Richard III, let alone a man like King David, can be convicted, from within, that what he is doing is an outrage, or the way in which a man like Luther can come to hold that the stand he is taking is a moral necessity. In other words, such reductionist accounts ignore precisely that feature of a person's conscience – its sovereign authority – on which Butler lays such stress in his careful depiction of the key elements in human nature. Such accounts inevitably tend to reduce authority to power in a way that strikes even the empirically minded, introspective, moral philosopher as implausible.

But how can Butler *explain* this feature on which he has put his finger? In order to answer this question we have to turn our attention to the implicit, and sometimes explicit, theology which undergirds Butler's ethical theory. At the beginning of Sermon II, Butler observes: 'If the real nature of any creature leads him and is adapted to such and such purposes only or more than to any other; this is a reason to believe the Author of that nature intended it for those purposes.' More specifically, Butler goes on to associate our being God's

[13] J. L. Mackie, *Ethics. Inventing Right and Wrong*, Harmondsworth 1977.

creatures with our being so constituted that virtue has a prior claim over any particular revelation.[14] W. R. Matthews, in a footnote to the first of these passages,[15] comments that Butler's formulation of the argument from final causes 'introduces the idea of an intelligent Creator', but goes on to say, 'It may be put without reference to a Designer. Aristotle uses the same idea when he argues that the true function of man is determined by his nature.' However, it is not so easy to bracket out such references to the Author of nature in Butler's text. For the feature of conscience in which we are interested, namely, its presiding authority and claim, is precisely that which cannot be accounted for by purely naturalistic teleological theories such as Aristotle's. Reference to our *true* nature, or to the *true* function of some element in it, point inexorably to the idea of our Maker's intention. The *authority* of conscience is a mark of our nature as God intended it to be. Thus we should take seriously Butler's characterisation of conscience, not only as 'moral reason', and 'moral sense' (Butler affirms both aspects), but as 'Divine reason',[16] as 'the guide assigned us by the Author of Nature',[17] and as 'that candle of the Lord within'.[18] Indeed, after bringing out the authority of conscience as its most distinctive characteristic, Butler insists that conscience 'if not forcibly stopped' (e.g. by self-deceit or indoctrination) 'naturally and always goes on to anticipate a higher and more effectual sentence which shall hereafter second and affirm its own'.[19]

It is interesting to compare this idea of conscience anticipating the divine judgement with Newman's celebrated 'exaltation' of conscience in *A Grammar of Assent*.[20] Newman, who was himself greatly influenced by Butler's writings, declares that 'the phenomena of Conscience . . . avail to impress the imagination with the picture of a Supreme

[14] Butler, Sermon I, para. 2.
[15] W. R. Matthews (ed.), *Butler's Fifteen Sermon and A Dissertation on the Nature of Virtue*, London 1958.
[16] Butler, *Dissertation*, para. 1.
[17] Butler, Sermon III, para. 5.
[18] Butler, Sermon X, para. 16.
[19] Butler, Sermon II, para. 8.
[20] J. H. Newman, *A Grammar of Assent*, London 1870, ch. 5, section 1.

Governor, a Judge, holy, just, powerful, all-seeing, retributive, and is the creative principle of religion, as the Moral Sense is the principle of ethics.' Butler is less overtly theological than Newman. He does not press this distinction between religion and ethics, still less between conscience and the moral sense. For Butler, conscience is indeed *our* moral sense and *our* moral reason, but precisely as such it is implanted by the Author of our nature and anticipates his final judgement.

Anscombe is able to disparage Butler's view of conscience only because she takes him to be talking about our fallible, purely human, moral sense. But this is to prize the subjective side of conscience apart from its objective foundation in human nature as the Author of nature intended it to be. That is why we have to think in terms of our *true* nature and its *intended* structure, if we are to do justice to Butler's ethical thought. That is why Butler's is a theological ethic, even if it is not a divine command theory. That Butler's is a theological version of natural law theory and not a divine command theory will be clear from the foregoing account, not least the reference to the priority of conscience and virtue over any particular revelation. It will be clear, too, why Butler prefaces both Sermons II and III with the same text – the classical natural law text – from Romans 2.14: 'For when the Gentiles, which have not the law, do by nature the things contained in the law, these, having not the law, are a law unto themselves.'

So, if we must urge against Szabados that Butler could not allow that conscience may tell a man to do the vilest things, we must urge against Anscombe that Butler has both an explanation and a justification for his exalted view of conscience. Butler's error theory concerning self-deceit, to which Szabados quite properly points, accounts for the phenomena which trouble Anscombe. But neither Anscombe nor Szabados is right to speak, with reference to Butler's thoughts, of a corrupt *conscience*, which may itself tell a man to do the vilest things.

This interpretation of Butler on conscience and virtue enables us to dispose of another accusation levelled against Butler's ethics, namely that it commits the naturalistic fallacy.[21] For Butler does not offer his account of conscience and virtue in human nature in purely descriptive, naturalistic, terms. On the contrary, *value* is built into his account from the very start. We are not given a description of human nature in neutral, value-free, terms, from which evaluative conclusions are then supposedly drawn. The authority of conscience, on Butler's view, is an evaluative principle already built into our nature. There is no way in which, without reduction, a value–neutral description of a human being can be given (such as Desmond Morris attempts, for example).[22] That is why we have to read Butler's depiction of human nature as an account of our *true* nature. Our true nature is to live virtuously, that is, benevolently, under the rule of conscience. To act in accordance with baser impulses, to put conscience to sleep, to let self-deceit prevail, is to live viciously, against our true nature, however 'natural' in another sense of that word,[23] it may be to do so. And there is no third, neutral, value-free, way between a virtuous or a vicious life. So Butler does not commit the naturalistic fallacy. In living virtuously we realise our *true* nature, as we were meant to be.

Alvin Plantinga has recently been exploring the notion of the 'proper functioning' of our cognitive faculties, in an attempt to sketch a theistic epistemology that overcomes certain basic recurring problems with secular, naturalistic, theories of knowledge.[24] It is interesting to ask whether Butler's treatment of our moral faculties can be thought of in a similar way. For Plantinga, a belief has what he calls 'positive epistemic status' – that is, constitutes a justified true belief and therefore *knowledge* – if and only if the cognitive faculties of the person holding that belief are functioning properly, i.e. as God intended them to do, in the environment for which

---

[21] See N. L. Sturgeon, 'Nature and Conscience in Butler's Ethics', *Philosophical Review*, vol. 85, 1976, pp. 316–56, and its refutation by T. Penelhum in his book. *Butler*, London 1985, pp. 61–70.

[22] E.g. D. Morris, *The Naked Ape*, London 1967.

[23] That other sense of 'natural' is explicitly mentioned by Butler in Sermon II, para. 6.

[24] A. Plantinga, 'Justification and Theism', *Faith and Philosophy*, vol. 4, no. 4, October 1987, pp. 403–26.

they were designed. This theistic epistemology, so Plantinga avers, succeeds in accounting for the possibility of human knowledge in a way secular epistemologies, relying simply on coherence or the responsible sifting of evidence, notoriously fail to do. Could we not say that, in the moral sphere, on Butler's account, a properly functioning conscience always succeeds in convicting us of wrong or prompting us to acknowledge the overriding claims of the good, since that is how the Author of nature designed our moral constitution? In both cases – the grasp of truth and the grasp of obligation – what guarantees success is our God-given nature fulfilling the Creator's intention. A further parallel between the epistemic and the moral cases lies in the common conviction, on a theistic world-view, that there is an intended fit between our faculties and their environment. Indeed, it is a feature of Butler's ethics that the world is so structured that virtue and cool self-love in the long run coincide. If we fulfil our true nature in living virtuously, that is, benevolently under the rule of conscience, we will ourselves achieve true happiness (though that should not, of course, become the *motive* of our action).

But the parallel between properly functioning cognitive faculties and properly functioning moral faculties is not exact. Our cognitive faculties can malfunction – say, through disease or the use of drugs. Certainly our moral judgements can go awry – through self-deceit or indoctrination, as we have seen. But Butler could not allow that conscience as such might lead us astray. In other words, Butler builds proper functioning into his very notion of conscience, in a way that belies the parallel between conscience and our cognitive faculties. In the epistemic sense, the divine guarantee only operates *if* our faculties are functioning properly; but in the moral case the guarantee is built into the faculty itself. That is why conscience cannot be thought of simply as *our* moral sense or reason. In the moral case, the relevant faculty is endowed with rightness and authority in a way to which there is no parallel in the epistemic sphere. When things go wrong in the moral sphere, it is not a matter of the malfunctioning of a faculty intended to work otherwise. It is rather a matter of the suppression or putting to sleep of a faculty which, if functioning at all, possesses a built-in guarantee.

This is the feature of Butler's moral theory missed by both Anscombe and Szabados in their treatment of Butler on conscience. Whether Butler is right is, of course, another story. But enough has been said to show that Butler's view of conscience stands or falls by its theological foundation.

4

The varieties of goodness

I

The topic of this chapter is very different from that of G. H. von Wright's 1960 Gifford Lectures, whose published title has been borrowed for its theme. 'By the Varieties of Goodness', said von Wright, 'I understand the multiplicity of uses of the word "good".'[1] By contrast, what is considered here is the multiplicity of ways in which human lives and human communities may be characterised as morally good.

Our topic clearly has much in common with what we have grown accustomed to calling 'ethical pluralism'. In the context of post-Enlightenment human ethics, ethical pluralism is thought of first and foremost as recognition and positive affirmation of the varieties of merely human goodness. The idea that there is a single, paradigmatic, ideal of human life, whether personal or social, is rejected. The conception of the highest good, the *summum bonum*, whether that of classical antiquity, of Augustine, of Aquinas, of Schleiermacher, or even of Kant, is denounced, sometimes vehemently, as Procrustean, by implication totalitarian, or at least failing to do justice to the great value of these very different forms of human life. Thus the American pragmatist, John Dewey, argued that the idea of the highest good was a menace to ethics since it denied the plasticity of human nature and impeded human enrichment and progress.[2]

In the context of comparative religious ethics, a similar interest prevails in the varieties of moral teaching and ideals

---

[1] G. H. von Wright, *The Varieties of Goodness*, London 1963, p. 8.
[2] J. Dewey, *Human Nature and Conduct*, New York 1922.

of life to be found in the different religions of the world. Whereas earlier generations of Christian scholars tended to disparage the moral systems of other faiths and to assume or argue for the ethical superiority of Christianity, now we find not only from students of religion but from Christian writers too a much more positive appreciation of the varieties of religiously motivated human goodness, and a refusal to 'grade' religions, whether for their moral or for their spiritual power. Thus John Hick argues that, so far as we can tell, all the great religions are 'equally productive of that transition from self to Reality which we see in the saints of all traditions'.[3]

Our primary concern, however, is neither with ethical pluralism as valued in humanist moral philosophy nor with the different religious value systems studied in comparative religious ethics, but rather with the common assumption that Christian ethics itself is a uniform discipline, that Christianity has one identifiable moral ideal, and that the *summum bonum* can be spelled out as a single paradigm. We will be exploring the varieties of goodness within the Christian scheme of things, and the question whether, in Christian ethics, moral perfection should be thought of as conformity to a unitary pattern. At the end we will return to the varieties of secular and other religious goodness, but still with a view to Christian theological evaluation of those phenomena; for Christian ethics must include a theology of all forms of human goodness.

There are, of course, other forms of human excellence than moral goodness. But we are not concerned here with the varieties introduced into human life by people's different roles in the community or by different forms of creativity and enterprise. Robert Adams has rightly pointed out that in Christian ethics, we are not to think that God is interested in moral perfection alone. The vocation to be an artist has a place in Christian understanding.[4] Our question, however, concerns not these varieties, but varieties of *moral* goodness. Of course, the pursuit of non-moral excellence raises moral

---

[3] J. H. Hick, *Problems of Religious Pluralism*, London 1985, p. 87.
[4] R. M. Adams, *The Virtue of Faith*, New York 1987, pp. 170f.

questions. The musician's vocation – or indeed the business-man's vocation – does not absolve one from the claims of morality. And we will have something to say about the way in which different roles and different vocations affect morality and its different forms. But our main concern is with the varieties of *moral* goodness within the overall scope of Christian ethics.

Adam's article, 'Saints', raises the interesting question whether sainthood, being primarily a religious notion, should not include exemplary participation in any of God's creative interests, moral or aesthetic. But he does not explore the possibility that God's *moral* interests may be various, giving rise to very different forms of moral sainthood and different forms of Christian moral community. Adams does, however, put his finger on the key factor that will enable us to investigate this possibility, namely, when he stresses that sainthood, moral or otherwise, is not so much a matter of following a pattern as of living in and from an ever deepening *relation* to the God who is the source of all good. It is this factor, the particular relation between the Christian and his or her God, that yields the varieties of excellence, including the varieties of moral goodness, in people's lives and in the communities they form.

The objection will be raised at once that classical Christian ethics *has* set a single pattern of moral goodness before us – the example of our Lord – and that the imitation of Christ does involve disciplined approximation to a particular revealed and normative ideal of human life. But, as has often been pointed out, the imitation of Christ cannot be thought of as a matter of 'uncreative copying'. Christ's unique salvific role is, of course, inimitable, and the particular circumstances of his time and place combine with those of his vocation to make him an implausible example simply to follow. Christian discipleship is rather a matter of relation – of growth in faith and love that permits the Spirit of Christ to work through us and build us up into Christian personalities and groups of very different kinds.

Certainly, there are some general features of the Christian life which we shall expect authentic followers of Christ to manifest in their lives. Paul spells these out in terms of the 'fruits of the Spirit' (Gal. 5.2f.). There will indeed be family resemblances between Christians, both as individuals and in community. But, despite these characteristic general features, we should not think of Christian men and women as, ideally, clones of Jesus. The saints are striking for their idiosyncrasy as much as for their manifestation of typically Christian qualities. Indeed, an ethic of character should stress not only the type of general qualities and virtues that, when habitual, come to constitute the Christian character – but also the individual personality, the unique 'character' in the other sense of that word, which is the product of an individual life story lived in and through particular and unrepeatable sets of inter-personal relations, including, supremely, the relation between that individual and his Lord. St Francis was evidently a Christian character in both senses of that word. But so are innumerable lesser figures whom any of us will have encountered in the course of our Christian journey and who will have helped us by their example – their example, that is, not only of general qualities such as forgiveness, patience, and love, but of particular and unique personal excellence and individuality of very different kinds.

It would be a great mistake in Christian ethics for us to follow the early Kierkegaard in restricting the sphere of the ethical to the general characteristics of good interpersonal relations and setting the individual off against that background as the bearer of a particular vocation that transcends or even suspends the ethical. On the contrary, the moral life is as much a matter of growth as a particular personality in relation to others and to God as it is of growth in the manifestation of the virtues. And there are many different ways of being a Christian moral individual.

The notion of 'works of supererogation' should be mentioned in this connection. A person may be inspired and enabled to go beyond the call of duty and dedicate their life to service of their fellows in a supereminent way – and in very different ways. When one thinks of Albert Schweitzer or of Mother Teresa of Calcutta, one is thinking of unique forms of the moral life that not only transcend ordinary goodness, including ordinary Christian goodness, but result in remarkably idiosyncratic moral characters.

We pointed out that the varieties of Christian goodness include not only very different supereminent examples, but also lesser and more ordinary, though equally individual examples. It is a mistake to expect sainthood of all. (Otherwise the notion of supererogation would be redundant.) As Voltaire observed, 'the best is often the enemy of the good',[5] and Christian moralists do the good – and the varieties of goodness – a disservice if in the interests of perfection they disparage the less striking forms of moral goodness. When Jesus said, 'You must be perfect as your heavenly Father is perfect' (Matt. 5.48), he was not setting up a quite impossible ideal for everyone to follow. As Keith Ward has shown, for a creature to be perfect (*teleios* in the Greek) is to fulfil one's end or goal.[6] God's unique and infinite perfection is, of course, realised eternally just by God being God, but ours is temporal, varied, and in any case only fully realised in the end. But what makes for Christian goodness, in both ordinary and extraordinary cases, is the actual relation to God in which the believer stands. As with all personal relations, each case is unique.

Affirmation of the goodness of moral lives at various stages of growth, and in innumerable less than perfect forms, helps us to see the point in the older 'idealist' teaching about my station and its duties.[7] Despite the apparently static and uncreative nature of such teaching, it at least involved the recognition that the moral life of the artisan, the civil servant, the businessman, the scholar, or the artist, entails special claims and obligations that themselves yield varieties of goodness.

To prevent the discussion becoming too individualistic, we will now explore an example from the basic form of human communal life – the family. Advocates of the imitation of Christ would do well to consider a good Christian marriage –

[5] Voltaire, *Dictionnaire Philosophique*, article on 'Art Dramatique'.
[6] J. K. S. Ward, *The Rule of Love*, London 1989, ch. 14.
[7] See, e.g. F. H. Bradley, *Ethical Studies*, Oxford 1876, essay V.

indeed the variety of good Christian marriages – as phenomena of the Christian moral life. Jesus himself, it seems, was celibate. But we no longer think of celibate Christians as ethically superior to married ones nor of the monastic life as ethically superior to the family. There are varieties of communal goodness here. But there are varieties within the varieties; for there is no one ideal pattern of Christian marriage. Not only are there different, particular, even idiosyncratic, good married relationships (as there are individuals), but also there are various possibilities, in part dependent on historical and social circumstances. It is not clear that there is a single set of ideal social circumstances in relation to which we should work out what an ideal Christian marriage should be like. Even if there were such a set, there might well still be different good possibilities – the extended family, the small family, the childless family, one partner working, both partners working, and so on. In each case, the Christian quality of the marriage would be a function of the partners' actual developing relation to each other, the other members of the family, society outside the family group, and of course, to Christ and his Church. For again, it is believers' actual and specific relations to their Lord that inform the moral quality of their common life, and these too will surely yield varieties of goodness.

But we cannot restrict attention to ideal social circumstances; for most of the time morality is a matter of how we live in very far from ideal circumstances, although, of course, it is also a matter of changing and improving those conditions. This is true of Christian morality as it is of any other sort. Christians anticipate ideal social circumstances in the fullest sense only in the end. We may well speculate about the varieties of goodness in the eschaton. But present less-than-ideal circumstances make for even more variety.

Let us stay with the example of family life and consider a question that came to prominence in the 1988 Lambeth Conference of Anglican bishops. Some bishops from Africa pleaded with the Conference to recognise the legitimacy in the prevailing circumstances of polygamy in certain types of

African society. It was not only unrealistic, but cruel to the actual women involved to insist on Christian converts renouncing all their wives bar one. No doubt the Church would continue to work for social change and for the replacement of polygamy by monogamy as the norm, but in the present less-than-ideal circumstances, could not a polygamous marriage and its extended family be regarded as good?

Not all less-than-ideal circumstances are social and in principle changeable conditions of human flourishing. It is widely believed that homosexual orientation is in many human beings a natural – in the sense of genetically based – condition. In these circumstances, it may be argued, a committed and faithful homosexual relationship is a moral good, and not to be condemned as if it were on a level with sexual promiscuity. When the singer Peter Pears refers to his life with Benjamin Britten as 'a gift from God' beyond desert,[8] not only the creativity but also the moral goodness of that relationship should be apparent to the Christian as to any moralist.

When we turn to consider wider forms of community life than those of marriage and the family, similar factors making for variety are to be recognised. We have already referred to the goodness of monastic life, not as a paradigm, but as one of the varieties. Indeed there are varieties of monastic life – all of them good. But the Church has fostered and encouraged many different forms of community existence and many different ways of contributing to the wider common good. Here, too, these varieties of goodness will in great measure be conditioned by the less-than-ideal circumstances that obtain. And the ways in which Christians, whether as individuals or as groups, will contribute to the betterment of those conditions are bound to vary greatly.

When Christians in the developed social democracies worry about the extremism and imbalance that seem to them to characterise many forms of liberation theology, black theology, or feminist theology, it is usually because they are thinking of Christian ethics in allegedly ideal circumstances

[8] In a television interview shortly before his death.

(often confused with their own), and not in relation to the actual conditions that have evoked these necessarily one-sided responses. Those who have visited and lived with a Latin American base community and come to appreciate the conditions and predicaments that have called forth these Christian communal responses have no difficulty in affirming their goodness. Of course, such forms of Christian community can constitute paradigms only in relation to extremely unideal circumstances. But, as already pointed out, the ideal circumstances will only be found in the eschaton.

The range of less-than-ideal circumstances is very great. Latterly, we have been speaking of extremely negative conditions that call for very special, and one hopes temporary, forms of Christian moral response at both the individual and the communal level. However, we should remind ourselves that much more positive social and cultural conditions will also be productive of very different moral personalities and groups. There is no reason at all why African or Indian Christianity should reflect Western cultural forms. In different cultures Christian contributions to the common good will exhibit diverse characteristics. Much work has already been done towards fostering local theologies rooted in particular historical and cultural situations.[9] Such theologies do not operate solely at the level of theoretical understanding or liturgical expression. Local theology is, in essence, practical theology.

A common feature of the circumstances making for the varieties of goodness in world Christianity is the universal fact of growth, development and change. The moral life is a function of the different stages in personal, communal, and social history. A recognition that perfection – itself possibly various – is an eschatological notion, together with a refusal to let the best be the enemy of the good, will under-gird our willingness to affirm the varieties of goodness, including the varieties of moral goodness, at every stage of life and history, in their manifold forms. There is much wisdom in Dietrich Bonhoeffer's treatment of the 'pen-

---

[9] See, e.g. J. C. England (ed.), *Living Theology in Asia*, London 1981.

ultimate' in his posthumously published *Ethics*.[10] But this notion of the penultimate needs to be greatly extended and diversified, if it is to do justice to the varieties of goodness.

Christian ethics has the flexibility to embrace and baptize these varieties just because its key category is not imitation but relation. One of the things that makes each individual person unique is the specific set of interpersonal relations that has gone into the fashioning of his or her life history. What makes a person, a family, or a community, Christian is their particular relationship to the Spirit of God and of Christ, in which they live and move and have their being; and this will differ in each individual case, at each stage of life and development, within each cultural context, and with respect to each set of circumstances. The point can, after all, be put in terms of imitation. Christ is exemplary precisely because his relation to the Father was so pure and immediate. Christ's perfection consisted in his dependence on and utter transparency to the Father's love and will. His commerce with the Spirit was unadulterated. But what that relation meant for him in his situation and with respect to his vocation was very different from what it means to Christian individuals and groups in very different circumstances, quite apart from the degrees of imperfection and adulteration that inevitably characterise our feeble approximation to that openness to the divine indwelling.

It may be helpful at this stage in the argument if we summarise the factors making for the recognition of the varieties of moral goodness in the Christian scheme of things. In the first place there is the recognition that morality is not simply a matter of types of action or types of motive, or even types of virtue and formed character. We have stressed the individuality, even idiosyncrasy, not only of the saints, but of each and every Christian man and woman as a moral personality. Then secondly, there are the many special interests and vocations, both moral and non-moral, of particular Christians. We referred to the varieties introduced into the moral life by people's different stations in life. In the third

---

[10] D. Bonhoeffer, *Ethics*, London 1955.

place, we must reckon with the impressive fact of works, indeed of lives, of supererogation. In the fourth place, there are the different circumstances that make for different modes of Christian interpersonal and community life. Some of these are positive, some neutral, and some negative. We referred to the less-than-ideal circumstances, some remediable over time, some not, but all making for varieties of Christian goodness, both individual and communal. But we also referred to cultural differences that yield different forms of excellence in Christian moral lives and groups. Fifthly, we mentioned the different stages in personal growth and historical development, yielding many penultimate forms of Christian goodness. Finally, and most important of all, we stressed the particular, living, relation, between Christians and the Spirit of their living Lord, that informs their individual and communal lives in very different ways as they seek to know and do God's will for them.

II

Two questions in particular will doubtless occur to those still wedded to the single paradigm of an ideal Christian moral life. The first concerns the possible incompatibilities and conflicts that may arise between the varieties of goodness all claiming the name of Christian. The second concerns the possibility and desirability of grading these varieties within the Christian fold.

We said that the different forms of Christian goodness will exhibit a family resemblance, recognisable in manifestations of the fruits of the same Spirit and in the effects of personal relation to the same Lord. There can, of course, be no compromise with evil nor any concession to contradictory values such as those of the vendetta or of racial superiority. But there will certainly be incompatibility and conflicts, not only in the obvious sense that one kind of Christian vocation necessarily excludes others, but also in the sense that in the less-than-ideal circumstances in which we find ourselves, some Christianly motivated choices and policies are likely to be at variance with others. Family resemblance is not denied by disagreement amongst members of the family. Some Christians, for example, will embrace pacifism, others will with regret endorse the just war or even tyrannicide. But who will deny the name of Christian either to Dick Sheppard or to Dietrich Bonhoeffer? The family resemblance is not abrogated by the fact of radically different choices. To adapt Sartre's famous example (which, as has often been pointed out, belies his own existentialist philosophy, since both options involve the recognition of objective claims) a young Christian Frenchman might well have been torn between staying to look after his ailing mother and going to work for the Resistance. Simone Weil, for example, took the latter choice. It is no part of Christian ethics to claim that there is always one right answer to such appalling dilemmas.

Christian ethical rigorists tend not only, quite correctly, to affirm that there must be no compromise with evil, but to insist that there must be no concessions to the less than ideal good. Thus Oliver O'Donovan writes that Christians, 'are called to accept exclusion from the created good as the necessary price of a true and unqualified witness to it'.[11] He says this explicitly with reference to those who may be 'ill-endowed psychosexually to enjoy the fulfilment and responsibility of sexual life in marriage'. But such rigorism may well be thought to confuse the supererogatory and the moral, and to fall foul of Voltaire's stricture about making the best the enemy of the good. A greater flexibility and compassion will allow us to recognise different kinds and levels of Christian goodness here as in other areas of interpersonal and social life.

The different levels of Christian goodness are not, of course, fixed or static. Recognition of, and rejoicing at, the many varieties of ordinary Christian goodness should be without prejudice to the possibility of extraordinary inspiration and growth – to the possibility, that is, of supererogation. To affirm the value of the good as well as of the best does not necessarily mean that we should rest content with the good.

This talk of different levels leads at once to the other question about grading the varieties of goodness within the

---

[11] O. M. T. O'Donovan, *Resurrection and Moral Order*, Leicester 1986, p. 95.

Christian fold. Clearly we do and must make such evaluations. The fact that the best should not be made the enemy of the good does not mean that the best is not better than the good. Lives like those of Albert Schweitzer and Mother Teresa are clearly closer to perfection than those of the good Christians we all know and love. To respond to a supererogatory call clearly takes a man or woman beyond the level of ordinary Christian goodness. But the facts remain that each level is good and that there are varieties of goodness at each level. We have already insisted that we ought not to grade the celibate against the married state or the Latin American base community against, say, a local group of the Society of Friends. And innumerable individual Christians at all levels are plainly incommensurable. So we have to be alert both to different levels and stages of growth towards eschatological perfection – here grading is possible – and to varieties of goodness at every level – here grading is not possible. And if, as hinted above, perfection in the end is not a uniform concept, then the consummation of all things will itself include ungradeable variety. The pure white of the divine light will for ever be refracted in the many colours of created being and goodness.

III

In the final part of this chapter, we return to the two subjects set aside at the beginning, namely ethical pluralism as valued in *humanist* moral philosophy and the different religious value systems studied in comparative religious ethics. We will consider each of these from the viewpoint of Christian theological ethics and in the light of our reflections on the varieties of *Christian* goodness.

Christian theology, except in its most extreme Protestant forms, has welcomed the fact and extent of ordinary human goodness as a sign and effect of the presence of God's Spirit in creation outside the Covenant. It goes without saying that recognition of the varieties of goodness within the Covenant will lead us the more easily to recognise the varieties of goodness outside. There should be nothing concessionary or grudging about this. On the contrary, not only are the varieties of secular goodness of great value in themselves – indeed sometimes reaching levels such as that of the secular sanctity portrayed in Albert Camus' Dr Rieux in *The Plague* – but they also can themselves come to form the basis of critique of distorted or mistaken Christian understandings of allegedly revealed morality. Ideally, – in theory, and, one hopes, often in practice – the relation between Christ and the Christian (mediated by the Bible and the Church), on which we have laid stress in characterising the roots of the various forms of Christian morality, should enhance and enlarge – and at times correct – the natural goodness of secular humanity. Sometimes, however, the reverse is true. Where Christian understanding has got warped or deceived, natural human goodness, itself the anonymous effect and reflection of God's goodness in creation, may help us to protest, and unmask the deception.

That consideration apart, much the same may be said about incompatibilities and conflicts between secular and Christian morality as was said in the case of the varieties of Christian goodness. Here too, we can make no concession to contradictory values. But here too, the best must not be made the enemy of the good. The different levels, and the varieties at the different levels, must be positively valued in themselves, but without prejudice to the possibility of further enlightenment and growth, both secular and religious. Certainly the Christian will hope and pray for the opening of his secular friend's eyes to the possibility of the Spirit's conscious indwelling and inspiration, but he will at the same time give thanks for the evident anonymous operation of that same Spirit already.

Finally, we turn to comparative *religious* ethics. There are similar points to be made in this connection. Again, Christian theological ethics cannot endorse contradictory religious values, but it can and must welcome other forms of religiously motivated goodness. Here it is a question of recognition of the way in which the Spirit has evoked *conscious* response, and of the forms of life, both personal and communal, that have developed in the different religious cultures. We may well speak of complementary values here. The Christian has no monopoly of the ways of God with humankind. There may well be forms of the religious life that encapsulate and manifest values understressed in the Christian tradition; and Christianity's historically dynamic and eschatologically orientated moral faith needs to be complemented by oriental cosmic wisdom.

At the same time, Christian theological ethics, valuing what it finds in other contexts, will want to let the Word of God in Christ be heard in and for those other contexts. We may have learned to look for what the unknown Christ, by his Spirit, has done and is doing already in the contexts of the other faiths; but we shall also want to let explicit forms of Christian life develop and flourish precisely there and in relation to those other histories, cultures and traditions. An immense range of fresh varieties of Christian goodness is opened up precisely by such processes of 'inculturation'.

If we ask whether the different forms of secular and religious goodness can be graded, our answer will be as before: some can and some can not. Christian ethics cannot renounce differential evaluation altogether. For all the wonder and value of the manifested forms of human goodness, some religiously informed, some not, Christianity's Christological vision and eschatological hope open up ethical dimensions of personal and communal living which it can only speak of in terms of enlargement, enhancement, or even sublation (*Aufhebung*). The negativities of the moral and religious life – the false values, the corruption, the horrors that human beings and human cultures have spawned throughout world history – are being deliberately set aside here. But the positive values whose worth we are concerned to stress can surely not all be placed on one level. We have already referred to the differences between the good, the better and the best. To take a religious example, Christian theological ethics must surely give a special place in the hierarchy of values to the Jewish forms of life, which provided the providential context of the Incarnation. As will be shown in chapter 7, Jewish conceptuality, sensibility, family life, and religious faith supplied the context and the vehicle of God the Son's incarnate life. The point has, of course, a key ethical dimension. Jewish morality was the form of life in which alone a perfect human life – that of the incarnate Son – could be lived on earth. The ethics of Jesus supervene upon Jewish ethics, and only very indirectly upon the whole ethical and religious life of humankind. It follows that Jewish morality must be 'graded' above all other forms of non-Christian goodness – good though they certainly are. And as far as Christian goodness is concerned, at this present stage in world history, it is best to refrain from making too many exalted claims, even for the saints. It is enough to say that, in the eschaton, it will be the explicit relation to God in Christ in which we shall all stand, namely, his conscious indwelling of us by his Spirit, which will sublate all forms of human goodness into the infinitely rich communion of saints (by then all will be saints) in the consummation of all things.

5

Divine and human goodness

In his *Ethics and Belief* – still the best short introduction to theological ethics from the standpoint of modern philosophy – Peter Baelz rightly observes that God's supreme authority is 'grounded in God's goodness and grace, not in his power'.[1] Very succinctly, he spells this out as follows: 'the Christian command to love is rooted in the conviction that God is love and that he has made man in his image'.[2] God's goodness consists in his nature as love; and his grace is his love in action. This ultimate reality is, of course, for Christian belief, no contingent matter. The very source and goal of all there is, is, in essence, absolute goodness and love. Whether we learn this from God's self revelation in the story of Christ and his cross, or deduce it logically from the basic premises of theism, God's goodness is necessary goodness, and his triune identity, as love given and received and shared still more, is necessarily what it is.

The divine goodness, spelled out in terms of love and of grace, is therefore the basis, the model, and the resource of all the myriad forms of finite, contingent, human goodness. As Christoph Schwöbel has argued, in an article on 'God's Goodness and Human Morality',[3] this is primarily a matter of relation. The divine inner trinitarian love is shared and mirrored by human beings in their relationships with each other (in family, in friendship, and society) and with God. In our own previous chapter, an attempt was made to show how

[1] P. Baelz, *Ethics and Belief*, London 1977, p. 88.
[2] Baelz, *Ethics and Belief*, p. 108.
[3] C. Schwöbel, *God: Action and Revelation*, Kampen 1992, ch. 3.

it is the unique pattern of interpersonal relationships in which a Christian stands with others and with God that gives each finite image of the divine goodness his or her individuality, whether of character of vocation, as the white light of the divine goodness is refracted into the myriad colours of the varieties of human goodness,

The suggestion that 'God is love' is not only a revealed truth but also, perhaps, a logical deduction, may have struck the reader as more than somewhat extravagant. In this chapter, we will be exploring this suggestion, and eventually defending it, through an analysis of the notion of divine goodness. The basic structure of the argument is this: logic constrains us to think of God as necessarily good. But there are problems in predicating goodness of God. Only the concept of God as love fully resolves those problems.

To call God 'good' is a paradigm case of analogical predication. The analogy is from human moral goodness. The problems with the notion of divine goodness arise from the limitations of that analogy. We discover that many important elements in the concept of human goodness cannot be transferred to God. We are driven to qualify the analogy (as we are, of course, with all analogies in our God-talk), but more so in this case, until all we are left with is love.

That the analogical base of talk of the divine goodness is human moral goodness should be clear on reflection. The goodness of God cannot be thought of simply as equivalent to his being. The sense in which *ens* and *bonum* are equivalent in their range, as the medieval doctrine of 'transcendentals' has it, is much too wide to capture the notion of the perfect goodness of the source and goal of all there is. As soon as we think of God in personal terms, as we are bound to do when we attribute mind and will to the Creator of the world, we have to think of God's perfect goodness as personal, moral goodness.

We will not be devoting much space to the first step in the logical argument outlined above – namely, the necessity of the divine goodness. This is most plausibly derived from the impossibility of an omnipotent and omniscient being doing evil. To accept this derivation is to side with Richard

Swinburne and Keith Ward[4] against Thomas Morris, for whom the necessity of God's goodness is more a matter of basic theistic intuition.[5] It is surprising the Morris, who has a remarkable penchant for undergirding traditional theism with logical argument, should confess defeat at this point. For surely it must be said that doing evil represents a deficiency in act or intention which omnipotent omniscience necessarily excludes. However, it is the next steps in the argument on which we will concentrate here. So whether God's necessary goodness is a matter of deduction, intuition – or revelation – we will simply take it as read.

The key elements in human moral goodness which we discover to be inappropriate for analogical transference from the human case to the divine, include libertarian freedom, duty and virtue. Let us examine each of them. Where human beings are concerned, our moral language only makes sense in the context of responsibility and freedom. But our freedom is the freedom to choose between good and evil. The condition of our growth in character and virtue is the possibility that we abuse our freedom and take the path of wickedness and vice. The reality, indeed necessity, of such a freedom is integral to any plausible theodicy. God permits wrong choices and the resulting havoc only because without such freedom created persons could not achieve their moral personality and identity. But we cannot transfer any of this to God in our analogical talk of God's freedom. God's freedom is not the freedom to choose between good and evil, if God is necessarily good. So what do we mean by the divine freedom?

God's freedom can only be thought of as the freedom to choose and enact the good, where no one course of action is the only possible good. God's freedom, in creation, in the manner of our redemption, in the innumerable modes of vocation and special providence, is the freedom of super-erogatory grace. And if, as suggested above, grace is love in

---

[4] See R. G. Swinburne, *The Existence of God*, Oxford 1979, pp. 97–102, and J. K. S. Ward, *Rational Theology and the Creativity of God*, Oxford 1982, chs. 6 and 8 .

[5] See T. V. Morris, 'The Necessity of God's Goodness', in his *Anselmian Explorations*, Notre Dame, Indiana 1987.

action, we are already on our way to supposing that God's necessary goodness must take the form of love.

It is worth repeating that it does not follow from God's necessary goodness and the mode of freedom that entails, that God must act in one way – namely the one and only best possible way. Supererogatory grace is under no such compulsion. There are innumerable ways in which God's grace will act creatively in the world. The necessity lies in *this* being the primary mode of God's free activity, not in the actual choices he makes.

Of course, there is an analogical base in human goodness for such a notion of supererogatory grace. Human freedom is not only exercised in choice between good and evil. Human beings image the divine goodness in their own derivative acts of supererogatory grace and love. And we look for an eschatological consummation in which the conditions of our formation are transcended and our perfected freedom approximates eternally to the divine freedom, in no longer being subject to temptation and abuse. So while the freedom which belongs to the conditions of our formation cannot be used in analogically predicated God-talk, the 'true' freedom of love in action which is sometimes glimpsed in human life on earth and is hoped for in the end in heaven, can be used as an analogical base for talking of God.

The second element in human moral goodness that causes problems for our understanding of divine goodness is duty. In our human case, duty is a matter of being bound by obligations which it is up to us to fulfil. If we do our duty we are commended as morally good; if we do not we are blamed. This conception of duty cannot be transferred to the divine case without qualification, since, if God is necessarily good, his actions will flow from his perfect nature without any constraint, let alone possibility of failure. The eternal God is not like Wotan in Wagner's *Ring*, who is torn mercilessly between his will and the treaties he has undertaken. In Wotan's sublime narration to Brünnhilde in *Die Walküre*, Act II, scene 2, Wotan cries out, 'These are the bonds that bind me. I became a ruler through treaties; by my treaties I am now enslaved.' Not so the Lord God of hosts, whose perfect goodness is expressed in all he wills and does without any conflict or constraint. However, the fact that in the strict sense, God can have no duties or obligations can be overstressed in a way which leads to a virtual denial of moral personality in God altogether. Thus Brian Davies, in his book, *Thinking about God,*[6] uses the fact that God is under no obligations as a way of dismissing the problem of evil. As the changeless, eternal and simple source of all there is, God is not to be thought of as a moral agent, to be blamed if he does not prevent the ills he clearly could prevent. God's goodness, on Davies' view, consists in metaphysical perfection, not moral goodness at all. Only if we think anthropomorphically about God do we find ourselves blaming God as Ivan Karamazov does in Dostoevsky's novel.

This type of theology, rooted in the Augustinian tradition though it is, has a disastrous effect on our understanding of the moral nature of God. It makes it quite impossible to think of God as love. For one thing, we cannot restrict morality to duty and obligation. As already noted, even in the human case works of supererogation belong to the moral life and afford analogies for our conception of God as love. But even duty can provide a certain analogical base for talk of God's goodness, as T. V. Morris has shown.[7] Morris argues that God necessarily acts in accordance with principles which for us specify duties. In our case a promise binds us with the obligation to fulfil it. God's promise entails necessarily his doing what he says he will do. So we can rely on God's goodness in a way analogous to human goodness, even in the sense of duty, But, of course, God, unlike Wotan, cannot want to do something other than what he has promised to do.

There is a sense in which we can speak of God's supererogatory acts of creating 'obligations' in God. We might say, for example, that it follows from God's decision to create a world of persons, that he is 'bound' to act redemptively to rescue them if they fall. Many theologians argue further for universalism in this way. Such obligations are not imposed on

[6] B. Davies, *Thinking about God*, London 1985.
[7] T. V. Morris, 'Duty and Divine Goodness' in *Anselmian Explorations*.

God from outside, nor is there any chance of his not so acting, given what he has already done. Such necessities are internal consequences of God's nature – perfect goodness. But again, it is only when we spell out that goodness in terms of love that we see how to hold together the analogies from works of supererogation and the analogy from duty. God's promises, which he is 'bound' to keep, reflect his nature to love. The consequential necessities such as promise-keeping, faithfulness, and so on, rest on the prior, free, creativity of love and grace. And there is nothing else they could rest on. Again we are constrained to spell out the nature of the divine goodness in terms of love.

The third element in human moral goodness that causes problems for our understanding of divine goodness is virtue. The importance of virtue and the virtues in any account of the moral life has been increasingly recognised in modern moral philosophy. In the human case, virtues are character dispositions, built up and rendered habitual over time, in a way which, as in the cases of freedom and duty, we cannot possibly transfer to our talk of the eternal and infinite Creator. Moreover, when we consider the four cardinal virtues and the three theological virtues, we realise that the majority of these are quite inappropriate for analogical God-talk. We may refer here to the excellent treatment of this matter by Philip Quinn in his book, *Divine Commands and Morality.*[8]

Take the four cardinal virtues, for example – courage, prudence, temperance and justice. It makes no sense to speak of God as courageous; for courage presupposes limited powers, real dangers, and genuine possibilities of loss, injury or death. It makes no sense to speak of God as prudent; for prudence again consists in the husbanding and direction of limited resources in the light of long-term goals. It makes no sense to speak of God as temperate; for temperance consists in restraint from yielding to immoderate desire. Only God incarnate can display these virtues, and it is *qua* incarnate, that is *qua* human, that Jesus lived courageously, prudently and temperately. Justice is, of course, different. Alone of the

[8] P. L. Quinn, *Divine Commands and Morality*, Oxford 1978, ch. VI.

cardinal virtues can justice be appropriately predicated, by analogy, of the divine. There is a great deal to be said in Christian theology about the nature of divine justice and in particular its relationship to God's love. We will return to this in a moment. But we should note at once that if we are to speak of something analogous to justice in God, it is in respect of God's relation to his creatures that we all call God just. Justice is hardly the right concept for thinking of God as he is in himself, in his inner-trinitarian relations. We do not suppose that Father, Son, and Holy Spirit manifest perfect goodness in acting justly towards one another. And if we are tempted to complain of some forms of atonement theology that the Father appears to be acting unjustly towards the incarnate Son, the answer must lie in correcting our theology of the atonement in ways which show not the justice but the love of God in the cross of Christ.

Even if we may speak analogically of the justice of God in relation to us sinners, this notion, being restricted to God's activity *ad extra*, cannot have the basic and prior status that we accord to the divine love.

Let us then turn to the theological virtues – faith, hope and love. Clearly, we cannot attribute faith to the absolute, infinite, and eternal God. It is controversial how far it is appropriate to speak of the faith of Jesus, God incarnate. There is a case for thinking it appropriate to see in Jesus' relation to the Father the paradigm of human faith. But again it is *qua* human, not *qua* divine, that God incarnate can be said to have exemplified, supremely, the virtue of faith.

Whether we can attribute hope to God depends entirely on whether it is correct to think of God in temporal terms. This is a highly controversial matter. If with Paul Helm[9] we defend the traditional atemporal conception of God's eternity, we can in no way predicate even analogically the virtue of hope of the divine. If, on the other hand, with many philosophers of religion, such as Swinburne, Ward and Lucas,[10] we find

[9] P. Helm, *Eternal God*, Oxford 1988.
[10] See R. G. Swinburne, *The Coherence of Theism*, Oxford 1977; Ward, *Rational Theology and the Creativity of God*; and J. R. Lucas, *A Treatise of Time and Space*, London 1973.

ourselves driven to postulate temporality in God in order to speak of him in personal terms and as a moral agent at all, then maybe there is some sense in which even the eternal God, having created an open-futured world, may have hoped that the path from creation to consummation might have been actualised less arduously than we know it to have been so far. Presumably the Holocaust was not inevitable. May we not suppose that God had hoped that his creatures would not persist in their depravity to such an appalling extent? The questions of theodicy that the Holocaust raises will not be pursued here, except to express the doubt whether anything remotely convincing can be said without appeal to an eschatological recreation and restructuring of torturer and victim alike, as Rabbi Dan Cohn-Sherbok has recently argued from a Jewish perspective.[11]

But even if we are able to predicate hope of God in some such analogical sense, we are still, as we were with justice, speaking of God's relations *ad extra* – namely to his human creatures and to the future of creation.

With love we come to the virtue which alone can be predicated of God not only *ad extra* but *ad intra* too. Human love, in its varieties and degrees, reflects not only the love of God for us his creatures but also and supremely the inner trinitarian relations of love given, love received, and love shared still more, that we glimpse through God's self-revelation in the mutual love of the Father and the incarnate Son, and their mutual indwelling by the Spirit, as well as the outpouring of the Spirit upon and in Christ's adopted brothers and sisters. Certainly, the winning and the transformation of God's personal creatures will entail what we can only speak of as the divine justice. Justice is how love is experienced by those yet to be transformed and indwelt by love. But, as Joseph Fletcher has rightly insisted, 'justice is love distributed'[12] (even if Fletcher's own conception of love leaves much to be desired). So we cannot set justice against love, and we must give love the priority.

[11] D. Cohn-Sherbok, *Holocaust Theology*, London 1989.
[12] J. Fletcher, *Situation Ethics*, London 1966.

Love is not just a matter of compassion, nor just a matter of self-sacrifice. Certainly, compassion is one of the forms love takes in relation to the suffering of sentient creatures. Certainly, we learn from the Cross of Christ that perfect love stops at nothing in the way of self-sacrifice in order to bring about the rescue of the lost and the unlovely from their predicament (whether self-inflicted or not). But love cannot as such consist in compassion or self-sacrifice, since in ideal conditions there would be no suffering, sin or loss, and love cannot depend upon there being such things in order to exist. This is clear even in respect of creation, whose eschatologically consummated state will surely not be deprived of love by the absence of death, mourning, crying or pain. *A fortiori*, when we think of God as being love in God's own, internal, trinitarian, relations, the impossibility of equating love with compassion and self-sacrifice is even more obvious. So both in the case of communion of saints in heaven and in the case of the blessed and glorious Trinity, love has to be *defined* otherwise, in terms of mutual self-giving, sharing, and rejoicing in the other's creativity and joy. As with supererogatory grace, so with its foundation, love, there is an analogical base in human experience – that of every anticipation of the future of creation given to us in ecstasty and mutual joy – but the prime analogue ontologically speaking is the mutual indwelling of the persons of the Trinity.

We return finally to the question of deduction and ask again whether and how far it is possible to deduce the fact that God is love – in this strong trinitarian sense – simply from the premise of God's necessary goodness.

Richard Swinburne has recently revived an ancient argument to be found in Richard of St Victor, to the effect that God *must* be thought of in trinitarian terms.[13] This *a priori* argument, in the earlier Richard at least, has two stages. First it is shown that God's goodness cannot lack the perfection of love, for nothing is better or more perfect than love, and without love there cannot be supreme goodness. Then secondly,

---

[13] R. G. Swinburne, 'Could there be more than one God?', *Faith and Philosophy*, July 1988.

the nature of love is analysed as necessarily containing both dilection and condilection. Dilection – *dilectio* – is love of another; condilection – *condilectio* – is mutual love of a third. In Swinburne's terminology, the values necessary to perfection must include sharing and co-operation in sharing. It is worth quoting Richard of St Victor, from his *De Trinitate*, on this latter point: 'In mutual love that is very fervent there is nothing rarer, nothing more excellent than that you wish another to be equally loved by him whom you love supremely and by whom you are loved supremely.'[14] There is perhaps a false step, as Swinburne points out, in Richard of St Victor's claim that a creature would be unworthy of such love. It is better to argue, more generally, with respect to both dilection and condilection, that the picture of God as love cannot possibly depend on there being creatures for God to love. The creation of a world of persons may indeed express and reveal God's supererogatory grace and love, but the world is not necessary to God, and we have to be able to think of God as containing within himself, prior to that creation, the perfection of love given, love received and love shared still more.

Both Richards – St Victor and Swinburne – have arguments against any further proliferation of persons in the Godhead beyond the three necessary to permit talk of both dilection and condilection in God. Without going into this in detail, we may note that the form of the arguments here is that, for Swinburne, there is no reason to postulate yet more persons in God since the necessary values of sharing and co-operation in sharing are secured by the three persons of the Godhead, and, for St Victor, unless we stopped at three, 'there would be irrationally an infinite processional series'.[15]

To sum up: the more we think about human goodness as the analogical base for talk of the divine goodness, the more we find ourselves driven to think of supererogatory grace and love as the most appropriate elements in perfect goodness for such analogical predication. Even justice, appropriate though

[14] Quoted from E. J. Fortman, *The Triune God*, London 1972, p. 193.
[15] Fortman, *The Triune God*, p. 194.

it certainly is, cannot be given priority over love; for justice is only one of the forms love takes in relation to finite creatures, who, unlike the persons of the Godhead, are potential competitors. But love can only be predicated of God as he is in himself, if we think in trinitarian terms of God as already love shared and shared again, before ever God creates yet more persons to enjoy the values of both dilection and con-dilection.

6

Does the doctrine of the atonement make moral sense?

There can be no doubt that we can, do, and must transfer *moral* notions, duly qualified, from the context of human interpersonal relations to that of divine–human relations. It is quite impossible, in the context of personal theism, still less in that of Christian trinitarian faith, to treat the goodness of God as an attribute of metaphysical perfection, unrelated to our human notions of moral goodness. On the contrary, if the divine goodness is to be spelled out, as it is, for a biblically based Christian understanding, in terms of love, the personal, moral, connotations of goodness must predominate in our thought of God's absolute goodness. As stressed in chapter 5 the analogical base for talk of God as good is human moral goodness, exemplified supremely, of course, in Jesus Christ, the incarnate Son of God (quite properly referred to as the human face of God), but not only in him; for the qualities of altruism, self-sacrifice, and unconditional positive regard, manifested in the life of Christ, are not peculiar or unique to him. Christ's supereminent moral goodness may enlarge, enhance, and indeed correct, our previous conceptions of what it is to be good, but we can certainly recognise its paradigmatic quality, and, in the light of Christ, note other lights at all times and places, that reflect something of that light. Nor is it only Christians who can do so. Christ's goodness was evident to Mahatma Gandhi, and is evident to many, uncommitted, readers of the New Testament.

Our understanding of the love of God – the divine *agape* – is gathered by analogy, from its incarnate manifestation and from any human story in which that love is reflected. It is this – and not some unrefined purely secular moral theory – that provides the basis for moral criticism of ideas and theories in theodicy and soteriology alike. When we say that God must have a morally sufficient reason for permitting suffering and evil in his world, it is this Christologically refined conception of the love of God that imposes the necessity of working out a morally convincing theodicy. And when we say, with John Hick, that the God of love revealed in the Christian Gospel cannot have restricted his saving encounter with humanity to a single strand of world history,[1] it is the same Christianly informed moral intuitions that require us to renounce exclusivism in the theology of religions. Similarly, moral criticisms of traditional theories of the atonement are most powerful when based on perceived incompatibilities between the love of God revealed in Jesus Christ and the particular theory or model in question.

Of course, we have to qualify the concept of moral goodness when we apply it, by analogy, to the infinite and absolute source of all other being and value. As argued in chapter 5, there are *a priori* reasons as well as revealed grounds for thinking that love alone can capture the supererogatory nature of God's goodness. It was pointed out there that we cannot think of God as subject to moral obligations in the way in which we humans are. But that recognition of the absence of any tension between duty and desire in the absolute goodness of God cannot be used as an excuse for absolving God from blame where the creation of a world containing evil is concerned. If God, for good reasons, creates a world that inevitably involves suffering and evil, then he 'must', by his own nature, accept and bear the responsibility for the inevitable risks and costs of creation.

Of all the doctrines of the Church, that of the atonement has elicited the most sustained moral objections. In itself, the idea that God has acted, decisively, to bring about the reconciliation of his wayward creatures with himself and with each other is very far from being open to moral objection. On

[1] See J. H. Hick, *God and the Universe of Faiths*, London 1973, ch. 7.

the contrary, it is of the essence of God's love to go out of its way to overcome evil and rescue God's personal creatures from the predicament and from the alienation in which they find themselves. It is to the models and theories which attempt to express precisely *how* this reconciliation was achieved that moral objection has been taken. Even St Paul's apparently unexceptionable summary of the gospel message – that God was in Christ reconciling the world to himself – raises the question of the moral propriety of such particularity. Why only 'in Christ'? And even St John's eminently moving summary – that God so loved the world that he gave his only-begotten Son that whosoever believeth in him might not perish but have everlasting life – raises not only the same question of particularity but a further question about the propriety of this concentration on *belief* in the Saviour. *A fortiori*, the particular models of the atonement, whether based on redemption from slavery, on propritiatory or even expiatory sacrifice, or on some purely juridical transaction, all strike us – or most of us – as morally dubious, at times morally outrageous. The moral dubiety or outrageousness centres on the notion of the death of Christ and its central role in atonement theories. How can the death of an innocent man count as a ransom and to whom was it paid? What sort of God requires propitiation by a death? How can the death of another expiate my sins? What sort of judge can impose death on another or even on himself as a substitutory punishment, thus letting me go free? Such ideas are morally objectionable in their analogical base – the purely human context – before ever they get transferred, by analogy, to the divine–human context; and, *a fortiori*, they make no moral sense when predicated of a God of love.

There is no doubt that forgiveness and reconciliation are deeply moral notions, and can indeed be predicated, by analogy, of the God who is Love. The question before us, however, is, can we really suppose that any forgiveness and reconciliation, and, *a fortiori*, God's forgiveness and God's reconciliation, depend on a death, the death of an innocent man, the death of God's incarnate Son? It was rejection, on moral grounds, of the idea that Christ had to die, before we could be forgiven or be reconciled to God, that led me to declare, some years ago, in the course of my response to *The Myth of God Incarnate*[2] (though here in agreement with its authors): 'It needs to be stated quite categorically that God's forgiving love does not depend on the death of Christ, but rather is manifested and enacted in it.'[3] If there was a necessity in the death of Christ, it did not lie on God's side; rather, that death was inevitable when perfect love became incarnate in a very sinful world. It was a virtual necessity from our side, given the depths of human wickedness. And such was the depth of God's love that he would not hold back from letting men do their worst to him, when he came among us in the person of his Son.

Such a view, admittedly, was unquestionably exemplarist, not just in the sense that the self-sacrificial love of God in Christ sets us an example to follow, but much more in the sense that the nature of God's costly forgiving love is exemplified in the life, passion and death of God incarnate. Of course, insistence that Christ's cross is God's cross in our world differentiates this position very much from that of *The Myth of God Incarnate* authors. Much is now held to depend on our being able to see the life of Christ, his passion, and his cross as God's own personal act of self-involvement. It made God morally credible, it was urged, if he were seen to be enacting his forgiveness in such a costly way. Among other things, we could see him taking on himself the responsibility for creating a world that was and is so vulnerable to sin and suffering. So the nature and depth of God's forgiving love are manifested and enacted in Christ's passion and death, but forgiveness was not made possible by the death. There was nothing in God himself – his justice, say – that required it.

Divine justice is often appealed to in support of traditional theories of the atonement. But justice cannot be regarded as an equally fundamental attribute for analogical predication as the attributes of love and forgiveness. Certainly we must suppose that God will treat his creature fairly. And certainly

[2] J. H. Hick (ed.), *The Myth of God Incarnate*, London 1977.
[3] Michael Goulder (ed.), *Incarnation and Myth. The Debate Continued*, London 1979, p. 94.

our sin cuts us off from the divine love. But there is no absolute requirement for retribution, nor, as we shall see, for reparation. Retribution, as one of Iris Murdoch's characters is made to say, 'is important as a check, it's necessary for the sort of rough justice we hand out here below . . .'.[4] It is precisely not transferable to the pure case of God's justice, which can only be thought of as an aspect of God's love. Reparation may be a good thing in the finite, limited, human context, but it is neither possible nor necessary in the context of our relations with God. In that context what matters, if reconciliation and salvation are to be achieved are (*a*) a forgiveness that does not cheapen or trivialise human sin, and (*b*) the transformation of the sinner into a healed and eventually perfected state of reciprocating love.

Certainly atonement is more than forgiveness alone and it might be argued that my treatment of the question in the debate over *The Myth of God Incarnate* was very one-sided in stressing the divine forgiveness to the neglect of what had to be done to make it effective in bringing about reconciliation. The aim was indeed to avoid the error of treating forgiveness casually in a way that trivialises sin. That is why the costly nature of God's self-sacrificial love, in coming amongst us in an incarnate life that involved the agony in the garden and the death on the cross was stressed. God's willingness to take all that upon himself revealed his forgiveness and his love in their full depth and extent, and rendered God morally credible. There is nothing casual or trivial about such love and forgiveness in action. But sufficient place was not, it seems, given to spelling out the other aspect of atonement, namely, what had to be done to make it effective in bringing about our reconciliation. Admittedly, atonement in the sense of at-one-ment or reconciliation appears no more to require a death than forgiveness does; but maybe atonement in the narrower sense of what had to be done to bring about reconciliation did make that death in some sense necessary. However, that would seem to bring us back to those unsatisfactory models, whether based on the sacrificial cult or

[4] Iris Murdoch, *Nuns and Soldiers*, London 1980, p 68.

on the theory of retributive punishment, that one found so morally objectionable and which seemed in no sense necessary in order to explain the effectiveness of God's love revealed and enacted by Christ in winning our response and refashioning us into union with himself.

For, after all, the effectiveness of the story of incarnate love in overcoming our impenitence had been stressed. Austin Farrer was quoted: 'What, then, did God do for his people's redemption? He came amongst them, bringing his kingdom, and he let events take their human course. He set the divine life in human neighbourhood. Men discovered it in struggling with it and were captivated by it in crucifying it.'[5] Once again it is God's own self-involvement to the point of dereliction and death that wins our response, but the death, as such, plays no indispensable constitutive role in alone making that response possible. That is how things worked out in fact, and that does win our response; but the forgiving love was there already, as was the response there already on the part of the disciples prior to the events of Holy Week. And there is no reason why reconciliation any more than forgiveness *had* to involve the cross.

Of course, there is much more to be said about sanctification and our conformity to Christ; and, given what did in fact happen, that more may be put in terms of dying and rising with Christ. But our death to sin and our rising again to righteousness are a metaphorical dying and rising. The reality is a spiritual transformation that is certainly necessary if we are truly to be reconciled to God. But again it must be said that the literal death of Christ plays no constitutive role in the bringing about of that transformation. Death and resurrection are, indeed, a necessary part of human destiny under God. But that general truth, to which Christ had to conform if the Incarnation was to involve a real human story, is not as such a necessary means of atonement.

In other words, justification and sanctification – the two elements in atonement – are best understood in terms of

[5] A. M. Farrer, *Saving Belief,* London 1964, p. 99.

God's free forgiveness and effective transformation of sinners, the moral seriousness of the former being shown in the whole story of the Incarnation, including the passion and way of the cross, and moral seriousness of the latter consisting in the fact that conformation to Christ is no easy, automatic transformation but a winning of our penitence and commitment by that incarnate love and an inspiration from within by the Spirit of that same Christ enabling us to become more Christlike in the Christian fellowship and eventually in the communion of saints. This may be regarded as objective a theory of atonement as we can hope for.

Let us now consider a number of recent theological and philosophical contributions to atonement theory to see whether any of them might suggest a revision of this view and lead us to acknowledge after all that atonement depends on the death of Christ.

First, we may refer briefly to two essays by Eleonore Stump: 'Atonement according to Aquinas',[6] and 'Atonement and Justification'.[7] In the first of these, Stump points out that, for Aquinas, the function of satisfaction is to restore a sinner to a state of harmony with God. Sins are remitted when the soul of the *offender* is at peace with the one offended. It is possible for another to make satisfaction for us, provided we ally ourselves with the substitution. The satisfaction in question is a humble, obedient, love present in suffering endured for others' sake. And the transfer is effected by God's sanctifying grace eliciting our response, as we commemorate Christ's passion in the Eucharist. It is interesting to observe that, although there is still some sense of artificiality in the way in which the language of satisfaction is still employed in this account, the morally objectionable aspects of the sacrifice model are entirely absent. In Aquinas's view, the transformation is entirely on our side. The sacrifice, with which by a kind of substitution we are associated, is characterised wholly in moral terms – a self-sacrificial offering of a life of obedient love – and the manner

[6] E. Stump, 'Atonement according to Aquinas', in T. V. Morris (ed.), *Philosophy and the Christian Faith*, Notre Dame, Indiana 1988, pp. 61–91.

[7] E. Stump, 'Atonement and Justification', in R. Feenstra and C. Plantinga (eds.), *Trinity, Incarnation and Atonement*, Notre Dame, Indiana 1989, pp. 178–209.

in which we are associated with it is also characterised in moral, personal, terms – God's sanctifying grace eliciting a sacramentally based response of a life of faith in the Christian community.

In her own account, in the second essay, Stump stresses the same key elements, this time without the artificiality to be discerned in Aquinas's retention of the terminology of satisfaction. Stump argues that justification by faith is a matter of our free acceptance of God's transforming grace. While allowing, as any morally serious account must allow, that this transformation is a gradual process, Stump presses the question how God effects the initial change in our will that opens up the transforming possibilities, without any over-riding of our free will. The wedge that cracks the heart and elicits conversion, she rather extravagantly writes, is Christ's passion and death, which she interprets as God's own self-sacrificial love in action. This is what atonement means in relation to justification by faith. It is thus that God undermines resistance, enabling God to reform the heart without violating it, and that, presumably, is what atonement means in relation to sanctification.

There is little in these essays that might threaten to overturn the view sketched above. Both elements in atone-ment theory are expressed in morally convincing ways. The 'wedge that cracks the heart' is God's own self-sacrificial love in action. And the inner transformation of us sinners is effected through a grace that builds up the life of faith. There are no inappropriate transfers of morally dubious elements in these accounts.

We turn now, again briefly, to Colin Gunton's book, *The Actuality of Atonement*,[8] in which the author attempts some-thing of a rescue operation on the classical models of the atonement by treating them as powerful metaphors for what God did and is doing in order to restore (or bring about) the original (or intended) harmony and moral order of his creation. Although Gunton subscribes to current views on the irreducibility of metaphor, he does, at times, attempt to

---

[8] C. Gunton, *The Actuality of Atonement*, Edinburgh 1988.

spell out, in non-metaphorical terms, the moral force of these traditional models. Thus, in the chapter on Anselm's satisfaction theory, he refers to P. T. Forsyth's insistence that 'the cross is God's way of so relating himself to human history that new relationships are both possible and real', and, in spelling this out further, writes, 'the cross is the place where God provides the means of the free forgiveness and sanctification of the sinner, without implying that the universe is an unjust place and that he is indifferent to moral realities'. The interesting thing about these formulations, morally unacceptionable as they are, is that they remain ambiguous between the view (to which both Stump and I would subscribe) that the forgiving love of God incarnate is enacted and exemplified in the passion and death of Christ, and the view to which, alas, Anselm himself appears to subscribe that reconciliation positively required that death. Indeed it seems that any attempt to extract the moral force of metaphors of the atonement will have the same effect of either ambiguously or deliberately detaching their moral significance from that allegedly objective necessity.

This suspicion is confirmed when we come to Gunton's chapter on 'Christ the Sacrifice: a dead Metaphor?'. The sense in which sacrifice is a living metaphor is, quite properly, referred back to Psalm 51's 'the sacrifices of God are broken heart . . .', and spelled out in terms of Jesus' sacrifice of a life of obedience 'even unto death'. Gunton stresses the key point that it is because God, through Christ's resurrection, takes up humanity into himself that we are not only forgiven but reconciled in a morally serious way. As Edward Irving puts it, 'the Son of God has given himself to be where we are, so that we might be where he is, participants in the life of God'. But once again these morally convincing formulations speak of the self-sacrificial nature of God's own incarnate love in the whole life of Christ and of the transforming, sanctifying, effect of the Spirit of the risen Christ in associating us with his permanent offering to the Father, as members of his body, the Church. The death, as such, plays no constitutive role here.

We shall now examine, at rather more length, Richard Swinburne's book, *Responsibility and Atonement*.[9] Swinburne's method in philosophical theology, in philosophical analysis, that is, of the meaning of Christian doctrine, is to analyse in meticulous detail the human conceptuality relevant to the subject area in question and then spell out its theological application. In this case he offers a close account of moral goodness, responsibility and freedom, merit and reward, guilt, atonement, punishment and forgiveness, and then, in the second half of the book, examines the application of these notions to our relation to God, namely to the whole question of sin and redemption.

As will be clear from the opening paragraphs of this chapter, there is no intention here to deny that this is a proper and fruitful method. We do indeed acquire our personal and moral language in the first instance from our forms of life in human communities where we interact as moral persons. This provides us with the relevant conceptuality with which to speak, by analogy, of God's love, God's justice, God's forgiveness, and what makes for reconciliation between ourselves and God.

Admittedly, a number of factors should make us wary of this method. For one thing the special, indeed unique, case of our relation to our Maker may well require, in part at least, a new vocabulary, designed to relate to those special circumstances. But it cannot be a vocabulary utterly divorced from our learned (and developing) moral vocabulary. As urged at the outset, the very fact that we find ourselves making moral criticisms of religious notions in atonement theory as in theodicy shows the necessity of maintaining contact between our moral intuitions and our religious doctrines.

But another danger of the Swinburnian method is that an error in moral philosophy is liable to lead to magnified anomalies in the theological context when transferred to the relation between God and ourselves.

So we have two problems: have we got our analysis of morality right, so that human error does not infect our

---

[9] R. Swinburne, *Responsibility and Atonement*, Edinburgh 1989.

analogical base? And are the analogical transfers appropriately made from the human case to the divine–human case, even where the moral intuitions do convince?

Much of Swinburne's account of the relevant moral concepts strikes me as accurate and illuminating. His defence of retributive punishment as the restoration (usually by the state on behalf of the victim) of the just equilibrium of benefits and burdens that was disturbed by the wrongdoer's act is controversial, as my quotation from Iris Murdoch will have shown, but this hardly affects our concerns here, since Swinburne himself rightly insists that there is no necessity in such redress, and hence the notion need not be transferred to the divine–human case, where the right – if it is a right – can indeed be overridden by forgiveness. Indeed, Swinburne is as critical, on moral grounds, of the penalty model for atonement as I am. The most dubious element in Swinburne's moral analysis, however, concerns precisely the notion of forgiveness. For he insists categorically that forgiveness can only follow repentance and apology and preferably reparation and penance too. (As we shall see, these are the four components Swinburne discerns in atonement.) Forgiveness, where there is no atonement, trivialises human life, says Swinburne. This is a truth, he claims, about human inter-personal life before ever its application to the religious context is made. But there is nothing trivial about the attitude evinced by the father of the girl killed in the Remembrance Day bomb at Enniskillen, when he said, 'I forgive them', just as there was nothing trivial about our Lord's word from the cross, 'Father forgive them, for they know not what they do'. And it seems that Swinburne deprives himself of the possibility of spelling out the deeply moral nature of God's self-sacrificial forgiving love, manifested and enacted in Christ's passion and death, which elicits the response of penitence and faith – which, in Stump's phrase, 'cracks the heart', enabling transformation to begin.

That is one problem with Swinburne's analysis. Certainly his analysis of atonement goes some way towards redressing the balance of that one-sidedness in concentrating on the divine forgiveness to the neglect of what has to be done before reconciliation becomes a reality. As mentioned just now, Swinburne holds there to be four components in a purely human act of atonement, leading to the restoration of relations broken or disrupted by wrongdoing. There has to be repentance, apology, reparation and penance. We may well ask why repentance and apology are not enough, whether as a response to forgiveness, on the view advocated here, or as eliciting forgiveness, on Swinburne's view. It is clear, in the purely human context, that, for serious cases of wrongdoing, repentance and apology are not enough. The harm of damage or wrong is often too great to be overcome simply by forgiveness, repentance and apology. In some cases reparation is indeed called for. Penance too may well be a mark of one's recognition of the seriousness of the wrong done. Sometimes indeed it may replace reparation where the latter is impossible. In the human case a penalty may have to be paid, either in addition to or in place of reparation. Often, however, the something more – in addition to repentance and apology – required by genuine atonement is not so much reparation or penance, let alone penalty, but amendment of life and the actual building up of the restored and renewed relationship that constitutes reconciliation. In many contexts, genuine costly forgiveness, leading not only to repentance and apology but to a process of amendment and reconciliation, may well involve the remission of penalty and the waiving of the right to reparation or of the offer of penance. The point to be stressed here is that in the purely human case we cannot insist on reparation and/or penance any more than penalty as a *sine qua non* of forgiveness and reconciliation.

Let us now consider the divine–human case. We have already commented on the oddness of Swinburne's insistence that divine forgiveness requires *prior* repentance and apology. That seems to fly in the face of the whole Gospel story. We must now focus attention on the oddity of what he says about reparation and penance in the context of our reconciliation with God. Swinburne holds that such is the seriousness of sin that repentance and apology plus forgiveness are not enough. There must be an equivalent of reparation and/or penance to mark the seriousness of the problem to be overcome and the depth of our commitment to the process of reconciliation. And here he calls upon the sacrifice model as a model which retains some moral force and enables us to give the death of Christ on the cross something of its traditional role as a necessary or central element in the once-for-all act of atonement. Unable to make a sacrificial offering of our own sufficient to fulfil the necessary task of reparation and/or penance, we are to plead Christ's perfect self-sacrificial act, made for us on the cross. By associating with this – through baptism – we are enabled to embrace the process of sanctification with the slate wiped clean.

This is a somewhat forced rescue operation, on Swinburne's part, of an element he mistakenly seems to think essential to the Christianity of the creeds. It is striking to find it in his quasi-credal list of theological assumptions.[10] Swinburne includes there, in his Christological clause, the belief that Christ's life and death were openly intended by him as an offering to God to make expiation in some way for the sins of men. This presumption – highly dubious as a piece of New Testament interpretation – seems deliberately designed to require what was referred to as the forced view of atonement as including necessarily *our* offering *Christ's* sacrifice as *our* reparation and penance. Despite Swinburne's intriguing analogies from ways in which parents may help children to make reparation for wrongs which they have done by providing them with the means to do so, this is surely not a morally persuasive, let alone necessary, way of regarding Christ's death. And the fact that Swinburne vacillates at this point between talking of our pleading Christ's sacrificial death and talking of our being associated with Christ's offering of a perfect human life to God the Father is another indication of moral and theological insecurity in this way of articulating a theology of the atonement. For actually the latter way of talking – of our being associated with Christ's offering of a perfect human life to God the Father – is a much more plausible way into a theology of sanctification and – to

[10] Swinburne, *Responsibility and Atonement*, p. 122.

repeat Bonhoeffer's phrase – of conformity to Christ. But on that view, Christ's *death* is not going to play the role in atonement theory that Swinburne wants it to do. For on that view, the something more, over and above repentance and apology, required for genuine at-one-ment, is not reparation and/or penance, but amendment of life and conformity to Christ through the sanctifying work of the Spirit of the risen Christ in our hearts and in our midst.

We conclude, therefore, in agreement with Stump, that the significance of the death of Christ lies more on the side of manifesting God's costly forgiving love than on the side of enabling our response, even though our response is in fact made by association with Christ's response, *qua* man, to that forgiving love.

What we have learned from Swinburne, as from Gunton, is the need to say much more about this response side of atonement theory and especially about the way in which our response, elicited by God's forgiving love enacted in the Incarnation and passion of Christ, is at the same time enabled by the perfect human response of the incarnate Son to his heavenly Father. The fact that this can be expressed, metaphorically, in terms of dying and rising with Christ is incidental to the moral realities of atonement.

In this connection, we may mention one more recent book, *Atonement and Incarnation*, by Vernon White.[11] The interest of this book lies in its attempt to defend the cosmic, universal, efficacy of the Christ event, not just its revelatory significance. This differentiates White's approach quite sharply from those of Stump and Swinburne, and, at least initially, from my own. For all of us, the Christian doctrine of atonement is a matter of revelation and response – revelation of God's costly forgiving love – and our response, whether of faith, reparation, amendment, or being gradually sanctified. Indeed Swinburne denies categorically what White affirms to lie at the heart of the Christian tradition, namely the universal efficacy of the Christ event, whether or not we consciously recognise it and consciously respond to it. Says Swinburne: 'If the sinner could

[11] V. White, *Atonement and Incarnation*, Cambridge 1991.

be forgiven as a result of Christ's death, without using it to secure forgiveness, we could be forgiven by God as a result of what happened on Calvary independently of our knowing about it.' The implication is that that would be absurd. Now we have already questioned Swinburne's understanding of forgiveness as requiring prior penitence and apology, and we have questioned the sense he gives to our using Christ's death. But we have not, so far, questioned the overall pattern of *revelation* and response as lying at the heart of what God did for us in Christ. White's book requires us to question even this. Intriguingly, and rather embarrassingly, he does so with the help of a quotation from a contribution to *Incarnation and Myth* by me, which at first I did not recognise or remember having made. White agrees that God's own self-involvement in the wicked world to the point of crucifixion gives God the right to forgive, but he goes on to stress that Christ's perfect response to the Father is itself not only revelatory but constitutive of our salvation, prior to our knowing about it. The quotation which surprised me is actually a cobbling together of three separate sentences, the last two of which were in fact a paraphrase of T. F. Torrance's view – hence the surprise and the embarrassment; for the significance of Torrance's basically Barthian soteriology had not been fully drawn out. It is Torrance and Barth who should really be cited as sources for White's theological insistence on the prior universal efficacy of God's salvific work in Christ. Be that as it may. Here is the quotation from *Incarnation and Myth* which White gives:

> The specifically Christian insight is that this too, the movement from creation to God, takes place in God, through the humanity of Christ, and derivatively through ourselves ... It is the incarnation which not only brings God to us but creates the conditions in which our own response to him can be made ... God incarnate also himself constitutes the perfect *human* response, by incorporation into which we are enabled to respond.[12]

---

[12] Goulder, *Incarnation and Myth*, pp. 95, 97 (quoted in White, *Atonement and Incarnation*, p. 56).

It is pleasing to be reminded that the response side as well as the revelatory side was stressed in that debate; but the basically Barthian point is that it is because God has done, in Christ's humanity, what we could not do ourselves that the salvation of all is in principle secured. It is not simply a question of God's own costly forgiveness, nor even of his securing the right to forgive, but of his enacting himself a perfect human response into which, one way or another, we and all humankind can and will eventually be drawn. There is, as Barth himself insisted, a genuine vicarious element here – even vicarious sacrifice – but not in the sense of penalty or expiation, but rather of a human self-offering to God which can become ours by adoption. The point to note, in contra-distinction from Swinburne, is that this is a matter, not of pleading the death of Christ, but rather of being incorporated into the incarnate and risen *life* of Christ. And this is a process that can, at least initially and to some degree, be thought of as taking place in hidden ways, prior to our conscious recognition. The point might, for instance, be developed into some theory of 'anonymous Christians'.

What is necessary, then, for our salvation is not so much the death of Christ as the Incarnation. Of course, God's own self-emptying is in fact carried through to the end – to the cross – and the depth of his forgiving love is in fact revealed there. By the same token, Christ's perfect human offering of his whole life, *qua* man, in fact culminates in the cross and is, in a sense, perfected there. But from neither side can we say that it is the death as such that effects salvation for the world.

Reflection on these recent contributions to the theology of the atonement reinforces the view expressed at the outset that some notions can all too easily be inappropriately transferred from the context of human interpersonal relations to that of divine–human relations. This is obviously true when those notions are already in the purely human context itself morally dubious or outrageous, as with many of the classical models of the atonement drawn from forms of life such as slavery and animal sacrifice already rejected and discarded on moral grounds. Other notions, such as retribution and reparation may retain some moral force here below, but make no moral sense when transferred to the divine–human case. There are some, more general, notions, like the particularity of the Incarnation which might at first seem scandalous, but which on further scrutiny are found entirely appropriate, as when the moral and religious significance of Christian incarnational belief is fully understood. There are other notions, such as love, forgiveness, supererogatory grace, and the sanctifying power of the indwelling Spirit, that enable us to speak in a morally convincing way of the atonement or reconciliation brought about by God's taking humanity into himself by the resurrection and ascension of his incarnate Son. We have seen that this involves a sacrificial self-emptying love that both renders God morally credible and wins our penitence and self-offering in return. And we have seen that our feeble response is then further enabled, sustained, developed and eventually perfected by the process of sanctification and assimilation to Christ's permanent offering of himself to God. Finally, we have speculated that the effectiveness of this process of assimilation may not be restricted to the sphere of conscious response to revelation and grace, but may well be anticipated and begun, universally, at hidden levels, as the Spirit draws all men and women to God through Christ before ever they come to realise that this is indeed their human destiny.

The task of the theology of the atonement is to rescue these spiritual truths that lie behind traditional atonement doctrine and express them in a morally convincing way.

Part Two

7

The Jewishness of Jesus

The task undertaken in this chapter is that of considering the significance for Christology of a relatively orthodox incarnational kind, of the fact that Jesus of Nazareth was a first-century Jew. In other words, the frame of reference taken here is the Christianity of the Christian creeds. The question asked is what the Jewishness of Jesus means for that. The task, no doubt, would have been much easier, though less interesting, had we followed the example of those who seek to demythologise the doctrine of the Incarnation, either in the interests of an eirenic global, pluralist, theology of the religions, or in the interests of a purely expressivist, anti-realist, analysis of Christian faith. Even on such views as these, as represented by John Hick and Don Cupitt, for example, there would be some interesting questions remaining: what still differentiates Christianity from Judaism? Why follow the Jewish prophet, Jesus, rather than some other? Does the Christian ideal necessarily retain its historical links with the Jewish ideal? But these are not the questions pursued here. It is not necessary to abandon the characteristic tenets of one's faith in order to make progress in inter-faith dialogue. Rather what we bring to the dialogue and submit to mutual questioning are the distinctive and representative faith-stances, true to the patterns of belief and worship of the majority of our co-religionists. So the question asked here is: What is the importance for Christian self-understanding of the fact that the eternal Son or Word of God became incarnate in and as the first-century Jew, Jesus of Nazareth?

The topic will not be pursued phenomenologically here. There will be no standing back from Christian conviction to consider, as it were from a neutral standpoint, what Christians in general might take to be the significance of the Jewishness of the one whom they believe to be God incarnate. The chapter is conceived as a Christian theological attempt to articulate theologically that significance. It is written from conviction that the doctrine of the Incarnation not only belongs to Christianity's essence, but is true.

Furthermore, it must be stressed that this chapter belongs in the field of systematic and philosophical theology, not the study of Christian origins. Historical questions cannot be avoided. Any interpretation of Christian doctrine has to stand the test of historical sifting of the evidence concerning Jesus of Nazareth. It is not that incarnational Christology must be *required* by the historical evidence alone, as Maurice Wiles suggests.[1] There are other factors than historical investigation which have led Christians down the ages to speak of Jesus as God incarnate. But incarnational Christology must be at least compatible with the historical evidence, and perhaps even suggested by it. For, certainly, the plausibility of the Christianity of the creeds is lessened if the best contemporary historical criticism is held to undermine that suggestiveness or that compatibility. The detailed historical argument is left to scholars in other fields, but clearly Christian dogmatic theology will have to include some plausible historical interpretation if it is to succeed in sustaining the view that, among other things, the Christian creeds speak of God's acts, indeed God's presence in person, in history. It will be the burden of this chapter to show that Christianity's conviction of a definitive *historical* incarnation requires it to take with the utmost seriousness the Jewishness of Jesus.

I

Let us begin by stating, in summary form, what it is not unreasonable to take to be the centre of the Christianity of

---

[1] M. F. Wiles, *The Remaking of Christian Doctrine*, London 1974, p. 18.

the creeds, the doctrine of the Incarnation. Christians believe that knowledge of God as the infinite personal and holy will behind the whole created order, knowledge long mediated by the developing faith of Israel, God's chosen vehicle of that knowledge's transmission, was once for all made concrete and specific by God's own Incarnation in Jesus of Nazareth. This bare affirmation needs some qualification, of course. Christians came to hold that only in one of the modes of his eternal being did God become man. God did not in any way cease to be God by coming amongst us as a human being. Indeed it was reflection on the Incarnation and on the relation between the incarnate one and his heavenly Father that confirmed whatever inkling there may previously have been that the one God of Israel had to be thought of as internally differentiated and related as love given and received.

Such an Incarnation, so Christians believe, did not, and could not have come out of the blue. It was long prepared through the history of Israel and development of her faith, so that the human vehicle of God's very presence in our midst was a first-century Jew, nurtured in the faith of Israel.

Nor was recognition of Jesus as God incarnate an obvious, easy, immediate affair. There was a long period of development from the initial reception – by some – of Jesus as the Christ, probably in response to the resurrection, perhaps before, right up to the Council of Chalcedon in 451, during which the doctrine of the Incarnation was hammered out in conflict with a whole variety of views, most of which came to be called heresies. Nor did the process end with Chalcedon. The Christian doctrine of the Incarnation has been reflected on and developed over the centuries, meeting new objections and assimilating new knowledge in religiously creative ways. A relatively recent example of such creative religious re-thinking – to be considered below – is the kenotic theory of the Incarnation.[2]

---

[2] See S. W. Sykes, 'The Strange Persistence of Kenotic Christology', in A. Kee and E. T. Long (eds.), *Being and Truth. Essays in Honour of John Macquarrie*, London 1986.

In order to bring out the significance which the doctrine of the Incarnation has held and still holds for Christian understanding, it is worth sketching five key religious ideas for which it is of crucial importance. The first concerns revelation. Specifically Christian knowledge of God, which is, of course, no more than a development of Israel's knowledge of God, is given its content, not through being told more about God, but through God's very presence in our midst in human form. The epistemological force of Christian incarnational belief is well brought out by G. F. Woods, in his book, *Theological Explanation*,[3] where, having argued in general for personal analogies for our talk of God – a point on which, presumably, Jews, Christians and Muslims would be happy to agree – he goes on to argue that what gives these personal analogies their particular precision is belief in the perfect humanity of Jesus as manifesting God to us uniquely in person. What it means for this view that Jesus was a Jew will be the main theme of this chapter. The present point is that, for Christians, the Incarnation is the culminating locus of divine revelation and controls their understanding of God's activity at all times and places. Much more could be said about *what* is revealed of God through the Incarnation. The relational, trinitarian, understanding of God that follows from reflection on God's gift of himself to us through Christ and the Spirit has already been mentioned.

In the second place, the Incarnation shows us God's costly, self-sacrificial, love in taking upon himself responsibility for the world's evil and bearing the brunt of it himself. The power of redemptive suffering was, of course, already known to Judaism, as in the Servant Songs of Deutero-Isaiah;[4] but that God himself not only feels but shares the worst the world can do, and thereby manifests in person his forgiving and reconciling love, is a central tenet of Christian belief. The religious power of the fact of the crucified God has been well brought out in the book of that title by Jürgen Moltmann.[5]

---

[3] G. F. Woods, *Theological Explanation*, Welwyn 1958.
[4] Isaiah 53.
[5] J. Moltmann, *The Crucified God*, London 1974.

In the third place lies the related point that the Incarnation furnishes us with the paradigm case of divine providence and thus gives us, so Christians hold, the key to interpret God's action in the world. More will be said about God's providence in what follows. Here is it simply stressed that the Incarnation shows conclusively that God does not act in the world by omnipotence directed in a straight line by omniscience, as John Oman put it,[6] but through a gracious personal relation. That grace is shown and encountered most particularly in the life of Jesus and in the way of the cross.

Fourthly, it may be pointed out that the Incarnation reveals not only God's nature but human nature too. God reveals what man was meant to be – that is, what men and women were meant to be – by being it. The fact that he was a man and not a woman is quite irrelevant to this. But the fact that he was a Jew and not of another people is important, as we shall see.

Fifthly, reference must be made to eschatology. For, according to Christian belief, humanity is permanently taken into God, Jesus is the human face of God for ever, and in the end, in God's eternity, it is believed that all men and women will be drawn to God by him. Again, the significance of the fact that God's *permanent* human face is a Jewish face will be discussed below.

II

Having sketched the content and significance of Christian incarnational belief, we now come to the main part of this chapter, in which the importance for this doctrine of the fact that Jesus was a Jew is explored in some detail. Our starting point is the doctrine of God's providence in history.

Austin Farrer has stressed the specific implications of this doctrine. In *Saving Belief*, he dwells on the fact that God incarnate could not be a 'man-in-general'.[7] 'In fact', says Farrer, 'he was a Galilean carpenter turned free-lance rabbi.' And in *Faith and Speculation*, Farrer links this point to the doctrine of

---

[6] J. Oman, *Grace and Personality*, Cambridge 1917.
[7] A. M. Farrer, *Saving Belief*, London 1964, p. 69.

providence. The paradigm of God's providence, he says, 'is Christ's ability to play his part with a mental furniture acquired from his village rabbi'.[8]

Providence is a key notion for both Judaism and Christianity. It was Israel's faith that taught us to see reality as history, a linear process moving under God's providence towards an eschatological consummation, and it was Israel's own history that was seen as specially providential. She, out of all the nations was God's chosen people, elected to be the special vehicle of God's self-revelation, a light to the nations. Christianity goes further in seeing Israel's history and faith as the necessary preparation for the Incarnation, the light to the nations providing the necessary context for the Light of the World. On Christianity's view, though not of course on Judaism's view, that light, focused finally in Jesus, God incarnate, ceases to be restricted to a particular, national, community as the vehicle of that light's transmission and becomes universally accessible to men and women of every race. But what it does not lose is its rootedness in the history and faith of Israel. The Light of the world is for ever a first-century Galilean carpenter, turned free-lance rabbi, whose teaching and example, in life and in death, was Jewish through and through.

The Jewishness of Jesus, in other words, is not contingent for Christian incarnational Christology. The fact that God could not become incarnate in man-in-general, but must come to us in and as a particular human being does not mean that any historical context and any race could have provided the necessary conditions for the Incarnation. On the contrary, Christianity insists that only *that* point in history and *that* people could provide the human vehicle for God's own personal presence in our midst as one of us. It had to be as a Jew that the Word was made flesh.

These reflections, of course, presuppose a serious belief in the reality of God. Moreover they presuppose a belief in God far removed from deism. A serious belief in providence sees the whole world process and the whole of human history as a

[8] A. M. Farrer, *Faith and Speculation*, London 1967, p. 103.

story of God's creative and providential work, shaping up a world of life and then so interacting with the human world as to fashion a particular type of religious consciousness that could express his – God's – own nature and will in human form. The interest of Christian incarnational Christology in the Jewishness of Jesus concentrates precisely on the fact that it was and is a Jew, equipped 'with a mental furniture acquired from his village rabbi' – to go back to Austin Farrer's words – who alone can and does incarnate God the Son.

It is worth pausing at this juncture to point out the folly of trying to distance Jesus overmuch from the Judaism of his day. Christian theology has often tried to stress what differentiated Jesus's teaching and understanding of his own mission from the various schools of Palestinian Judaism in the early decades of the first century. No doubt to some extent this is an inevitable and important enterprise; for the story of Jesus did indeed lead to a new universal, incarnational, trinitarian, religion, breaking away from its parent body. But the fact remains that it was Judaism that made its offspring possible and supplied the categories for this development. Moreover, Christian incarnational Christology itself, as has been pointed out, requires the rootedness of the Jesus movement in Jesus the Jew. So it is counterproductive to insist too strongly on the difference. It is particularly counterproductive if the alleged historical reconstructions so distance Jesus from Judaism as to make him historically incredible, quite apart from the regrettable tendency among Christian apologists to denigrate the Judaism of Jesus's day.

Consequently, the Christian theologian will take an interest in attempts, whether from the Jewish side, as with Geza Vermes,[9] or from the Christian side, as with Ed Sanders,[10] to show, with historical verisimilitude, the Jewishness of Jesus. To repeat, it is not intended here to try to adjudicate on such historical interpretations. But it is worth quoting Sanders' remarks on the implausibility of an allegedly Christian reconstruction, such as that of Ernst Käsemann, which, says

---

[9] G. Vermes, *Jesus the Jew*, London 1973.
[10] E. P. Sanders, *Jesus and Judaism*, London 1985.

Sanders, 'is basically opposed to seeing Jesus as a first-century Jew, who thought like others, spoke their language, was concerned about things which concerned them and got into trouble over first-century issues'. Sanders continues: 'It is thus bad history. Though I am no theologian, I suspect that it is bad theology.' It is quite clear that Sanders is no theologian, but it is equally clear that the theology he castigates *is* bad theology. For Käsemann's theology does make Jesus an historically incredible figure, and precisely for that reason makes nonsense of the Christian understanding of God's providence, if that providence does in fact reach a climax in a genuinely historical incarnation.

We have not yet finished with the doctrine of providence; for the other side of Farrer's insistence on the paradigmatic nature of Jesus's ability to fulfil his providential role with a mental furniture acquired from his village rabbi is recognition of the necessarily hidden and mediated character of God's providential action up to and including the Incarnation. At no point does God force his self-revelation upon us. As in creation, so in providence, God limits himself to what Kierkegaard called 'indirect communication',[11] letting his nature and will gradually become apparent to religious minds, nurtured in a particular community of faith, and acting in and through the history of that tradition without – in Farrer's words again – faking or forcing the natural human story.[12] Not surprisingly, it gets written up in quasi-mythical form, with many miraculous divine interventions, but we learn to apply an element of demythologisation as we school ourselves to read the story historically and to interpret the history in terms of what is essentially a non-miraculous understanding of divine providence. We discover the theological importance of indirect communication. It makes more theological and religious sense to see God's action not as overriding the human story but precisely in and through the all-too-human story. It is, in fact, a *moral* necessity to retreat from blatant interventionism in our interpretation of salvation history. We

---

[11] S. Kierkegaard, *Philosophical Fragments*, ch. 2.
[12] A. M. Farrer, *A Science of God?*, London 1966, p. 78.

cannot seriously assert a direct divine teleology behind the battles and famines. But once we have made that strategic retreat, we begin to see how much more religiously powerful is a doctrine of divine self-limitation and of mediated providential action.

At every level, creation and providence involve divine self-limitation and indirect communication. There is a natural scientific story to be told about cosmic evolution and the emergence of the various forms of life, culminating in rational personal beings such as ourselves. Thus God creates us in and through the structures of matter, which he respects as he fashions our being. There is a natural human story to be told about the history of religions and the emergence within it of a particular form of ethical monotheism in a people conscious of the holiness and grace of God, aware of the possibility of redemptive suffering in their own history and destiny, looking for the coming of God's kingdom of justice, peace and love. Thus God evokes and fashions the context of his own most special self-revelation in an incarnate life, which opens up for all mankind a new saving encounter with the God of the whole earth.

The self-limitation and indirect communication involved in a real historical incarnation has, in recent centuries, been spelled out in terms of the kenotic theory. The idea of divine kenosis, or self-emptying, has an immediate moral appeal. By humbling himself and coming amongst us as one of us, the divine Word or Son lives out a genuinely human life, experiencing what it is to be a human being, knowing grief and pain and dereliction from within. Once again God does not overwhelm us by direct intervention. The human vehicle of his personal presence, action, and indeed passion, is a real human being. The moral force of this conception of the divine kenosis has already been mentioned in the course of our initial sketch of the significance of the doctrine of the Incarnation. But kenotic Christology is more than a morally powerful piece of anthropomorphism. It is a metaphysical necessity, that if God is to come amongst us genuinely in human form, then such self-limitation must take place.

Kenotic Christology is not to be thought of as involving the abandonment of divine attributes, nor, as David Brown, in his book, *The Divine Trinity*,[13] suggests, as an alternative to Chalcedonian two-natures doctrine. On the contrary, God remains God, and the divine Son or Word remains the divine Son or Word, in living out this particular human life and revealing the divine life by subjecting himself to genuinely human experience. But incarnation involves kenosis for all that, since the human vehicle of the Son's incarnate life is indeed a man growing in knowledge, ignorant of many things, and a member of a particular race and family.

In connection with kenotic Christology, too, it is important to stress the Jewishness of Jesus. For the genuine humanity of the incarnate Lord did not only have to be particular, limited and historically and culturally conditioned, as all humanity is. It had to be thus limited in the specifically Jewish way in which Jesus's humanity was limited. For only a Jew, with a Jew's inheritance, a Jew's faith and understanding and a Jew's hope, could be God incarnate. That faith alone could sustain the very image of God's being. It was, so Christians believe, for that purpose that God, in his providence, fashioned the Jewish way of being human and the Jewish way of being religious.

Of course, Jesus did not know that he was God incarnate. St John's meditations on the great mystery of the Incarnation cannot be read back literally on to the lips of Jesus. No real human being could know that he was God incarnate. So, if God, in the person of his Son, was to become incarnate in and as a real human being, it must have been in and as a man who did not know that he was God incarnate. Only the utter and transparent openness to God and dependence on God that Jewish faith made possible for a man could mirror and be, humanly, God's 'very self and essence all divine', this side of the divide between Creator and creature. Recognition of his divinity could only come later and somewhat arduously in and through another all-too-human story, by which God providentially evoked and fashioned the faith of the Church.

[13] D. Brown, *The Divine Trinity*, London 1985.

High Christology of the kind defended here must be very careful to avoid the heresy of docetism. But it is crude and primitive thought which denies to Jesus a human mind or a human personality. On the contrary, it is not just Jesus's *human* mind and personality that manifest God to us salvifically; it is Jesus's *Jewish* mind and personality that manifest God to us salvifically. The only truth to be discerned in the old doctrines of anhypostasia and enhypostasia is that Jesus of Nazareth, in the perspective of incarnational Christology, is not an independent purely human individual, co-opted or adopted by God for a particular function. In the providence of God his human, Jewish, person, spirit, or subject is through and through the vehicle of God the Son's incarnate life. There is a personal identity there, unique and pivotal to all God–man relations in the history of creation. But that does not mean, as has often been affirmed in classical Christology, that Jesus was not a human person. He most certainly was. Indeed he was a first-century Jew. But that human person, that first-century Jew, was, so Christians believe, God incarnate. The ultimate subject of his words and deeds was God the Son; but God the Son spoke and acted not only in but as the Galilean carpenter, turned free-lance rabbi.

Kenotic Christology, in its turn-of-the-century British rather than its nineteenth-century German phase, was rightly concerned with the consciousness of Jesus – its limitations and its growth, with Jesus's ignorances and misconceptions, as well as his insight, depth, and moral and religious creativity. The doctrine of kenosis may be seen as a way of reconciling, theologically, a high doctrine of the Incarnation with the quest for historical verisimilitude necessitated by the rise of the historical critical method and its application to the Gospels. But insufficient attention was paid at the time to the Jewishness of Jesus's consciousness. The tendency was to stress what differentiated him from Judaism. Only now, with the greater interest that has been shown in recent decades, from both Christian and Jewish scholars, in Jesus within the context of Judaism, are we in a position to evaluate theologically the importance of Jesus's Jewish consciousness for a doctrine of divine self-presentation and revelation in and through an historically believable natural human religious story. And at the same time Christian theology is enabled better to recognise the providential indispensability of precisely that form of religious consciousness – the Jewish – as the vehicle of God's incarnate presence.

Another Christian theological motif illuminated by concentration on the Jewishness of Jesus is that of the uniqueness and unrepeatability of the Incarnation. A striking feature of Thomas V. Morris's book, *The Logic of God Incarnate*,[14] is its defence not only of the coherence of the doctrine of the Incarnation but also of the theoretical possibility of multiple incarnations. If the divine mind of God the Son could contain the human mind of Jesus without being contained by it, so, in theory, could other minds, terrestrial or extra-terrestrial. Each could in theory express in finite human form the person who God is. Morris does not hold that there have been multiple incarnations, only that there could be. But his admission of the theoretical possibility shows that he has not grasped the full significance of the Christian doctrine of the Incarnation. For it is not simply the channelling of the divine mind through a human mind that constitutes incarnation. The divine Person of God the Son is channelled through and expressed in the whole personality of Jesus, the first-century Palestinian Jew. Everything that went into the making of his Jewish consciousness – the whole history of Israel – is essential to the providential formation of that unique incarnate life. I have argued elsewhere the more general point that two or more human beings could not *be* God incarnate, without splitting God's personal identity.[15] This point is now reinforced by recognition of the embeddedness of Jesus's personality in the whole religious inheritance of his people. Jewishness was constitutive of the human person he was and is. This makes God's human face – to use again this evocative phrase – necessarily and for ever a Jewish face and indeed this particular Jewish face. The idea of multiple incarnations, then,

[14] T. V. Morris, *The Logic of God Incarnate*, Ithaca 1986.
[15] 'The Uniqueness of the Incarnation', now reprinted in B. L. Hebblethwaite, *The Incarnation. Collected Essays in Christology*, Cambridge 1987, pp. 49–52.

falls foul of three things: first, the very concept of personal identity; second, the specific cultural formation of a particular person; and, third, the permanence of personal identity through all eternity.

It is important to spell out here this notion of cultural relatedness in the formation of a human person. It may have seemed that this discussion has concentrated too narrowly on Jesus as an individual. His Jewishness may have been stressed, but clearly, on the view defended here, it is this particular man who is the incarnate Son of God. There can be no going back on that idea, since personal being is indeed focused in individuals and we are rightly suspicious of the notion of corporate personality, except as a metaphor. But, for all that, a whole set of interpersonal relationships goes into the making of a human person. Jesus of Nazareth was no exception, and, if he was and is God incarnate, then his people's history, his Jewish culture, and his actual relations with Mary and Joseph, the village rabbi, and the disciples went into the making of the human person God incarnate is. Those who suppose that God might appear on earth from time to time as a whole series of individuals have simply not thought through what being a human individual involves, nor have they thought through what kind of human religious consciousness can alone carry and express the divine nature.

III

Before we turn to consider a major objection to the kind of kenotic theory of the Incarnation that requires rather than belies an historically realistic portrayal of the Jewishness of Jesus, let us attempt to sum up the view advanced so far. We have deliberately set out to explore the significance of the Jewishness of Jesus from the standpoint of Christian credal orthodoxy and in particular from that of incarnational Christology. We began by giving a brief account of the doctrine of the Incarnation and of why it is held to be so central and important in Christianity. Five points were stressed – the revelatory significance of the Incarnation; the way it shows God taking upon himself and bearing the brunt of the world's evil; its crucial exemplification of the manner of God's providence; its disclosure of what a human being was meant to be; and finally its eschatological significance as the permanent and final focus of God–man relations. Turning to the theme of providence, we pointed out how a real Incarnation required the special providential preparation, within the history of religions, of a community and a faith capable of both constituting the matrix and providing the particular human vehicle for God's incarnate presence in our midst. It was suggested that it was the peculiar features of Judaism that performed these functions and that therefore the Jewishness of Jesus was of the essence of the divine–human person that he was. It was also suggested that the embeddedness of the incarnate one in this particular context reinforced our intuition of the inevitable uniqueness of the Incarnation, already apparent from reflection on the nature of personal identity.

Now throughout this presentation the indirect and mediated nature of the operation of divine providence in preparing and bringing about the Incarnation has been emphasised. At no point need we resort to literal belief in miraculous intervention. In the person of Jesus, as in the history of Israel, God certainly intervenes, but he works in and through the historical and the human, without faking or forcing the natural human story. On this view, the Jewishness of Jesus is not contingent nor is it transcended. On the contrary it is precisely Jesus the Jew who is the human face of God. Kenotic Christology, it was suggested, positively requires us to stress both the historical verisimilitude of Jesus's life and teaching within the Judaism of his time and the specifically Jewish character of his message, his self-understanding, and his action.

A major objection to this highly Kierkegaardian stress on indirect communication and the divine incognito in such a kenotic theory of the Incarnation is this: how can the divinity of Christ be held to be *revealed* if it is at the same time held to be *hidden* within the humanly credible story of Jesus the Jew? This is the most acute example of a more general difficulty with the concept of non-miraculous special providence which we have taken from the writings of Austin Farrer and attempted to develop. If the hand of God working in and through the natural human story, without any faking or forcing, is, as Farrer claims, 'perfectly hidden', how can the story be recognised as providential and thus revelatory of God's nature and will? In fact Farrer had a very definite answer to this very understandable question. The hidden hand of God is detectable retrospectively in the light of its *effect*. This is true throughout the whole creative process. The hidden hand of God behind cosmic and biological evolution is recognised in the light of what has emerged from cosmic and biological evolution – a world of life and of rational and personal beings. The hidden hand of God behind the history of religions – here we are extending the argument, since Farrer did not turn his attention to this problem – is recognised in the light of what it has produced, the plurality of life-enhancing faiths. The hidden hand of God behind the history of Israel is recognised in the light of the special relationship with God which it created, expressed, as it was, in the covenant faith, the sense of vocation, the ethical and spiritual profundity, including the idea of redemptive suffering, and the eschatological hope. The hidden hand of God behind the life stories of particular individuals, prophets and saints and many lesser figures too, is recognised in what God makes of people's lives in and through the contingencies and vagaries of circumstance. Many people have looked back over a sequence of apparently meaningless events and discerned a providential pattern in what has emerged from them.

When we turn back to the Incarnation, a similar claim may be made. The providential intelligibility of all that went into the making of Jesus Christ is seen in its effect and first of all in the remarkable moral and religious quality of Jesus's teaching and example. Much stress is rightly being placed on its Jewishness. Only Judaism could have nurtured the free-lance rabbi and charismatic healer of the gospel narratives. What Jesus made of his Jewish inheritance, however, is undoubtedly more than just a striking synthesis. It was something new and creative, strongly suggestive of special providence at work. But, although Jesus's teaching and action and example are suggestive of God's providence, they could not by themselves have given rise to Christian incarnational belief. Certainly it is possible to interpret the Incarnation as the climax of God's providential action. The Incarnation itself can be thought of as the high point of God's indirect communication, as, without breaking the structures of his creation and indeed precisely by fashioning a natural human home for his incarnate presence, God, in the person of his Son, presents himself within those very structures in human form. But the Jewish prophet, Jesus of Nazareth, for all the wonder of his teaching and example, would never have been recognised as God the Son incarnate, without an event which did indeed break natural continuities, which did indeed transcend the historical, and disclose retrospectively, albeit only after much reflection and experience, the divine nature of that Jewish prophet's person. In the case of Jesus, when we attempt to assess the providential significance of his life in the light of its effect, we encounter something that cannot be assimilated to the notion of providence. What brought about the Christian movement, including its growing discernment of the divinity of Christ, was not just the story of the life and teaching and death of the Jewish prophet, Jesus, but the resurrection.

The New Testament narratives concerning the resurrection of Jesus are notoriously difficult to handle historically. The ancient historian, Michael Grant, can only point to the stubborn evidence of the tomb's being found empty and to the previously disillusioned disciples' belief that they had seen the risen Christ alive after his death.[16] The Jewish historian, Geza Vermes, in reporting this astonishing development agrees that probably the tomb *was* found empty, and holds that early Christian belief in the resurrection was just one among several interpretations of this disconcerting fact.[17] The more or less agnostic Protestant historian, Ed Sanders, while recognising the unique effect of the resurrection experiences of the disciples, confesses that he has no special explanation or rationalisation of them.[18] The Christian theologian,

[16] M. Grant, *Jesus*, London 1977, ch. 10.
[17] Vermes, *Jesus the Jew*, pp. 37–40.
[18] Sanders, *Jesus and Judaism*, p. 320.

Maurice Wiles, bending over backwards in his attempt to give an historically plausible account of the resurrection experiences that does not require the postulation of special providence, let alone a new creative act of God, can only resort to the psychologically implausible, reductionist, view that the appearances were visions expressive of the disciples' new-found conviction – itself unexplained – that Jesus was, after all, vindicated by God.[19]

From the standpoint of a relatively orthodox Christian theology, the historians' inability to render the resurrection intelligible comes as no surprise. And, sympathetic as he may and should be to the portrayal of the life and work and teaching of Jesus in historically credible terms, the Christian theologian really has no interest in rationalising or demythologising the resurrection. For it is the resurrection of Jesus from the dead that creates the possibility of finding in the (on any view) remarkable story of Jesus the incarnational significance summarised in the Christian creeds, the moral and religious force of which was spelled out at the beginning of this chapter. It creates too the possibility for the Christian to 'encounter' Jesus as a living Lord in prayer and sacrament. These are what was hinted at earlier when it was said that more than historical factors have led Christians down the ages to speak of Jesus as God incarnate.

We must now consider another objection that may be pressed from the Christian side against what may appear to be the rather complicated, kenotic incarnational theology defended here. Indeed the theology is even more complicated than has been suggested, since the full trinitarian implications of the theology of God, which incarnational Christology requires, have not been spelled out. But surely, even the Christian objector may say, one does not have to impose all these theological complications upon the wilting shoulders of the faithful. What inspires the faithful is not the kind of theology or Christology offered here, but rather the gospel story told in simple form age after age. This is what moves people. And its power to move people is only obscured by the

---

[19] M. F. Wiles, *God's Action in the World*, London 1986, pp. 90–3.

kind of theology expounded here. One of the great attractions of the current vogue for 'narrative theology' is its refusal to get detached from the biblical stories as the primary vehicles of faith.

The reply to this objection is that there is indeed a valid insight in the recognition of narrative as the raw material of theology. For if the incarnational theology is right, then God incarnate on earth was an itinerant rabbi or prophet, the story of whose words and deeds puts us in touch with God incarnate as he was during his earthly sojourn. Moreover, it is the human story of the God-man that expresses the divinity to us. Once again we come back to the Jewishness of Jesus and to the fact stressed all along that it is Jesus the Jew, in his Jewish context, who reveals God to us most intimately just because he – that Jew – is God with us, Emmanuel. Moreover if asked to say *what* the Jewishness of Jesus consists in, one does not try to abstract certain typically Jewish characteristics, one simply tells the gospel story.

But the theology is required as well, if we are to be able to interpret that human, Jewish story as God's own story of Incarnation. In the so-called Christian centuries this need was latent. For one thing, in the gospels themselves, the story is already theologically saturated, and, for Christians in the Church, the credal framework was universally taught and presupposed. Actually this had a rather bad effect in overlaying the historical Jesus with more or less docetic, unhistorical, constructions. The revelatory force of the humanity – the Jewish humanity – of Jesus was lost behind the time-honoured theological projections. The rise of historical criticism has enabled us to recover, to some degree, the authentic human figure of Jesus the Jew. But while this helped to recover the heart of revelation – the actual figure whose story brings God home to us in person – the fact that it was God's own story easily gets lost if the theology is jettisoned. Without the theological framework, it will cease to be apparent why this Jew from nearly two thousand years ago, remarkable though he was, is still determinative of our understanding of God and of our relation to God now and for all eternity. In other words, what we need in Christian theology is a high Christology which does not distort the human – Jewish – vehicle of God's self-revelation through incarnation. That is the purpose of a kenotic Christology which sees the point of the divine incognito and of the indirect communication of God's very self and essence all divine – to use Cardinal Newman's words once again – in and as a Galilean carpenter turned free-lance rabbi. We have suggested that such a theological framework is both made possible and required by the resurrection of Jesus from the dead, experience of which opened the eyes of the disciples, and opens the eyes of all who encounter the risen Lord, to the real identity of this Jewish prophet. So, while Christian incarnational Christology requires the historical, thoroughly human, Jesus as the revelatory and salvific locus of Christian faith, the historical, thoroughly human, Jesus by himself, uninterpreted by the resurrection faith of the Church, cannot be thought capable of sustaining Christianity. It is only *qua* God incarnate that that remarkable Jew, Jesus of Nazareth, is of universal significance and can be seen to be of universal significance.

⚘

8

A critique of Don Cupitt's Christian Buddhism

Numerous references in *The Sea of Faith*[1] and in later writings indicate the appeal and sense of kinship which early Buddhism – Theravada Buddhism – has for Don Cupitt. It is not only in the Buddha's hostility to metaphysics and the sense that religion does not require a metaphysic that Cupitt finds a kindred anti-realism. In the book, *Life Lines*, Cupitt remarks that realism has 'an itch of egoism about it whereas the non-realist easily learns a Buddhist lightness and good-humour in the use of religious externals'.[2] This link between realism and egoism – to be questioned later in this chapter – may be contrasted with the Buddhist 'no-self' doctrine, itself compared by Cupitt with the deconstructed, decentred, hyper-relativism of the forms of 'post-modern' philosophy which he, somewhat surprisingly, embraces as cognate with his own view of religion. Moreover the sequence of images, myths, and constructed 'life-worlds', in terms of which we picture our-selves, and between which we have to choose, is like an album of photographs, and 'there is something very Buddhist about a photograph', says Cupitt.[3] The comparison between early Buddhism and post-modern French philosophy is pursued further by Cupitt in *The Long-Legged Fly*,[4] where he takes the Buddhist quest for the cessation of desire to be a matter of

---

[1] D. Cupitt, *The Sea of Faith*, London 1984.
[2] D. Cupitt, *Life Lines*, London 1986, p. 123.
[3] Cupitt, *Life Lines*, p. 192.
[4] D. Cupitt, *The Long-Legged Fly*, London 1987.

rooting out erroneous conceptions of the self and of combating egoism and possessive individualism.

There are limits to Cupitt's enthusiasm for early Buddhism, however. He does not find in Buddhism the positive ideal of self-giving love, which is Christianity's contribution and which still inspires even an anti-realist Christian faith. Buddhism, indeed, teaches a selfless non-attachment, light, unburdened. But, as Cupitt observes in *The New Christian Ethics*,[5] the Buddha rejects all desire, and has no thought of making history. Again in *Life Lines*, Cupitt says, 'Just to will the death of God is atheism, and just to recognise and accept the Void is Buddhism; but to accept that for Love's sake, one must die in union with the god is Christianity.'[6] So, while Cupitt shares the Buddha's hostility to metaphysics, admires the way in which he prefigures post-modern deconstructionism, agrees with his negation of the self and its egoistic desires, and applauds his lightness of touch and freedom from the external trappings of religion, Cupitt prefers, embraces and commends a Christian ideal of selfless love.

We will not attempt to assess the accuracy or plausibility of Cupitt's understanding of early Buddhism, though it is far from clear that the Theravada is in fact as anti-metaphysical as Cupitt thinks. Furthermore, a case could be made for thinking in much more positive terms of Buddhist disinterested compassion, so that the difference between Christianity and Buddhism, ethically speaking – the difference, that is, between love and compassion – might not be so very great, and, consequently, Cupitt's preference for Christianity over Buddhism might be somewhat arbitrary. But staying for a moment with the question of metaphysics, let us consider a somewhat different reference to Buddhism in the work of another critic of objective theism, Alistair Kee. In an essay entitled 'Transcendence and God: A Critique of Religious Objectivism',[7] Kee remarks upon the resonances between Karl Jaspers' philosophical faith – the insistence on

[5] D. Cupitt, *The New Christian Ethics*, London 1988, pp. 61ff.
[6] Cupitt, *Life Lines*, p. 130.
[7] A. Kee and W. T. Long (eds.), *Being and Truth. Essays in Honour of John Macquarrie*, London 1986, pp. 62–84.

non-objectifiable transcendence which Kee makes his own –
and Buddhism. Now there are subtle differences between an
existentialist insistence on non-objectifiability in talk of
transcendence or in talk of God and Cupitt's explicit rejection
of theological realism. It would be possible to read the Buddha
and Jaspers and the mystics to whom Kee also refers as
exemplifying not so much a rejection of metaphysics as a
recognition of the unsayable – of the way in which any attempt
to state the truths of ultimate reality inevitably falsifies what is
beyond human, finite, conceptualisation. Whether or not this
is what Kee has in mind, such a view is vulnerable to Cupitt's
bluff assertion that the emperor has no clothes. Fear of
falsification through objectification can all too easily lead to a
complete rejection of philosophical and theological realism,
not only in respect of God or the transcendent, but also in
respect of science, anthropology, and culture. The question
whether Kee's position can, in the end of the day, be
differentiated from Cupitt's is a question which reflection on
the latter's extreme anti-realism presses upon us. The same is
true of the question whether D. Z. Phillips's insistence on the
autonomy of God-talk in the context of religious forms of life
can in the end be differentiated from Cupitt's anti-realism.[8]

This chapter is not so much concerned with Buddhism
itself as with Cupitt's own anti-realism. For, over the years, in a
series of books which manifest a rapidly changing and
developing philosophical and religious position – developing
inexorably, however, in a particular direction, so that it can
still be call a 'position' – Cupitt has thought through, as
consistently and resolutely as it is possible to think through, a
way of understanding the ethical ideals and spiritual
disciplines of Christianity as not only possible for one who
categorically rejects belief in an objective God and in life
after death, but as requiring such a rejection. But Cupitt's
purely humanist, expressivist, and voluntarist understanding
of Christianity is not simply a matter of being a non-realist
in religion. It is bound up with a much wider anti-realism,
with a Heideggerian reading of the history of philosophy as

---

[8] See D. Z. Phillips, *Faith and Philosophical Enquiry*, London 1970.

culminating in the death of metaphysics with an allegedly Wittgensteinian reduction of ontology to language and linguistically constructed 'objects' and 'life-worlds', and with a post-modernist Derridaean deconstruction of all essences, including the human self and its inherited cultures and life-ways. The novelty of Cupitt's position is the way in which, from the ashes of all this destructive criticism, there emerges, Phoenix-like, the Christian ideal of disinterested love, as something inspiring and demanding, a creative project that stands out amongst the innumerable other possibilities in the post-modern supermarket as eminently worthy of choice and commitment. Moreover this ideal and com-mitment to this ideal can, for Cupitt, still be expressed and enacted in the traditional language and liturgies of the Church, even though their meaning has been systematically translated out of theological realism into the vehicle of an anti-realist faith.

In the main part of this chapter, Cupitt's anti-realist position will be subjected to criticism, first for its religious in-adequacy, second for its intellectual inadequacy, and, third, for its ethical inadequacy.

We begin with its religious inadequacy, since one of the difficulties facing the philosopher of religion in commenting on Cupitt's views is that Cupitt is liable to sound much more religious than his critics. (The same difficulty occurs for critics of D. Z. Phillips's views.) To turn from Cupitt's passionate advocacy of an anti-realist faith to the meticulous work, say, of Alvin Plantinga or Richard Swinburne in the philosophy of religion may seem to be a matter of turning from the living heart of religion to a dry-as-dust intellectual world of abstrac-tion and theory. On a superficial view, we might seem to be renouncing Jerusalem in favour of Athens. And it might seem more than just churlish in the Christian critic to speak disparagingly of the evidently powerful faith and spirituality that inform Cupitt's writings. However, it is surely incumbent upon men and women of religion to reflect not only on the sense of their religious position – its inner sense and the sense it makes of everything else – but also on precisely what it is that constitutes its religious plausibility and power. We cannot simply take it on trust that the religious plausibility and power of Christian spirituality remain the same when the language and liturgies of the Church are re-interpretated in a non-realist way – that is, without reference to an objective God or life after death.

For the heart of the Judaeo-Christian tradition, from the Bible to the present day, has been a matter of discovery and experience, in communal as well as in individual life, of a *relation* between believers and an all-surpassing personal and spiritual resource, experienced both transcendentally and immanently, that creates, enables and sustains their faith and spirituality. In order to test the adequacy of Cupitt's reconstruction, we have to ask what sense he makes of Christian talk of *grace*. As far as one can see, the only sense he makes of it is in terms of the sheer gratuitousness of the faith possibility. Like wonder at the beauty of the earth, religious faith amazes us and becomes an inspiring possibility for us out of the blue. But Cupitt can hardly speak of amazing grace. He can only speak of amazing faith as a gratuitous possibility in human life.

Much could be said of the difference, phenomenologically speaking, between traditional Christianity's understanding of faith and spirituality in relational terms as expressive of a relation of dependence of believers on their God and Cupitt's one-dimensional, non-relational, understanding of the community of faith. But phenomenological arguments alone will not suffice in a critique of Cupitt's position. Cupitt is well aware that his understanding of Christianity is different from that of the majority of his co-religionists throughout history (although he makes some rather extravagant and implausible claims about what theologians since Schleiermacher have 'really' meant). Cupitt thinks that Christianity's self-understanding must change radically, and he has a theory based on his reading of the history of philosophy of why it must change. (Similarly, phenomenological arguments are to no avail against Cupitt's interpretation of Theravada Buddhism. The fact that Buddhists would not accept Cupitt's understanding of Buddhism is neither here nor there. For Buddhist self-understanding too, must change.)

In pointing out the difference between Cupitt's non-realist reconstruction of Christian faith and the traditional realist, relational and dependent faith of the Church, we are not, therefore, simply making a phenomenological point. We are questioning, rather, the religious adequacy of a view which abandons these key features of biblical, as of credal Christianity.

The first question that arises is whether such an anti-realist view could ever hope to sustain a Church or a world religion. It might inspire a few heroic individuals; but surely it could never have created the Christian movement or have maintained it as a world religion, fostering the simple faith of millions as well as the sanctity of such as St Francis or Mother Teresa today, and succouring at all times the broken and the outcast. Even at the most humdrum level, it is hard to see how one could realistically expect to have a congregation of existentialists or anti-realists.

This may seem just a sociological point. It is an empirical fact that it was faith in God that created the Christian movement (as it did Islam), and it is an empirical fact that these religions are sustained by faith in God. But it is more than that. The sociological fact is secondary to and dependent on the soteriological fact that an anti-realist faith cannot save us from our sins. This remark need not be taken in any narrow pietistic sense. The point is rather that it is a quintessentially Christian insight that God alone – God, that is, in his surpassing spiritual power, the power, however, of self-sacrificial love at the heart of all reality – can effect the necessary transformations of human life, both at the individual and the social levels.

It is easy to reply that ideologies as such can change individuals and effect major social transformations. Marxism is a case in point. The phenomenology of conversion to Marxism is strikingly similar to that of religious conversion; and Marxist ideology has transformed many societies radically – perhaps more radically than Christianity has done. But this assimilation abstracts from the realities of religious experience. Conviction of and commitment to the inevitable historical triumph of socialism is one thing, Christian experience of grace quite another. The former is a deliberately secular, this-worldly, reading of the dynamics of human history. The latter is inextricably bound up with its reference beyond history to a transcendent spiritual power. Once admitted to be a purely human construct, the Christian vision loses its power, except for a small elite. Actually, even Marxism needs to be sustained by conviction of historical inevitability. Once that is demythologised, Marxism too, tends to lose much of its power. So in fact the assimilation goes the other way. But the point about Christianity's religious power depending on belief in the reality of grace remains.

The case of Buddhism again might seem more appropriate to mention at this point than that of Marxism. For early Buddhism is the classical example of a *religion* that exerted striking spiritual power and sustained the faith of millions, without appeal to God, grace, or an enabling transcendent/immanent spirit. But the actual history of Theravada Buddhism should give the anti-realist some pause. A case can be made for thinking that its virtual demise in India and its development into Mahayana Buddhism in the Far East reveal a degree of religious inadequacy in the original austere ethic and spiritual discipline. It is hardly coincidental that what replaced Buddhism in India was a renewed devotional theism and, in part, a renewed metaphysical theism, and what developed in the Far East was precisely a religion of grace.

Another religious inadequacy in Cupitt's anti-realist faith may be discerned if we consider the exigencies of worship. In Christian worship the infinite source and goal of the whole creative process becomes the explicit focus of the creature's adoration, gratitude and praise. The creature is drawn out of himself or herself, not into the Void, but into an express articulation of that absolute dependence on the God who made the world and predestined human beings for eternity. Worship, as Peter Geach has pointed out, is an intentional verb; and much has been said about what constitutes the proper object of worship. The dangers of idolatry, of absolutising the finite, and getting caught in what Paul Tillich categorises as the demonic, all reinforce the religious sense that only the transcendent, infinite love of God can be appropriately worshipped and adored. In a non-realist faith all this goes. This is not to say that it is replaced by idolatry – though the danger of absolutising and objectifying our own ideals is there. What seems to happen in Cupitt's case, rather, is the commandeering of the language of worship for purely expressive purposes. Worship loses its intentionality.

Some attention must now be given to Cupitt's charge that a religion of dependence on an allegedly transcendent power is bound to be an immature affair. This basically Freudian objection – at the root of so much protest atheism – suffers from immense implausibility when confronted with the facts of the religious life. It is difficult to know whether it has become a purely *a priori* theory imposed upon the facts whatever they are, or whether it is just a wild generalisation induced from a small range of experienced cases of indubitable religious immaturity. But one of the problems with Cupitt's extremism is that it makes him wholly indiscriminate in his judgement of traditional religion. Something is surely wrong with a theory that prevents its holder from distinguishing, even empirically, between mature and immature religious believers. But the theoretical disadvantages of the view that all religious dependence relations entail immaturity are equally great. One ceases to be able to explore with any sensitivity the kind of theological anthropology which sees in our creaturely, dependent, status a defining attribute of what it is to be a human being. Of course, much depends on the way in which this relation of dependence is understood. It can be affirmed slavishly, blindly, or immaturely. But the religion of grace, worship, and discipleship is not necessarily experienced in those inadequate ways. Rather, the mature Christian learns the meaning of true freedom through embracing the will of the God who is love, and letting his or her heart rest in the God who made us for himself.

The religious inadequacies of the anti-realist view can be summed up in the charge that it fails to do justice to religious experience. This means that there is an argument from religious experience to the reality of God. The widespread occurrence of a religious sense of encounter with a transcendent/immanent spiritual reality behind and at the heart of things – ranging, as it does, from a sense of absolute dependence, through numinous experience of various kinds, to a sense of standing in a gracious personal relation to the God and Father of our Lord Jesus Christ, constitutes a prima facie case for theological realism. Such an appeal to experience provides the basis for John Hick's apologetic in his debate with Michael Goulder in the book, *Why Believe in God?*[9]

Three points may be made about the appeal to religious experience, two positive and one negative. The positive points are these: in the first place, it is worth noting that the argument from experience is an argument. So already, before leaving the topic of the religious inadequacies of an anti-realist faith, we are involved in its intellectual inadequacies. It fails to account for religious experience of the reality and grace of God. Then secondly, it is important to remember that the more specifically rational considerations to which we are about to turn are to be held in conjunction with the appeal to experience. It is the same ultimate reality to which reason appeals as that to which religious experience appeals. There is no need to drive a wedge between the God of the Bible and the God of the philosophers. The philosophers are only exploring the rational side of the case for accepting that to which the religious sense gives prima facie plausibility.

The negative point about appeals to religious experience is that they are unlikely to convince by themselves – unless, of course, one has oneself enjoyed what strikes one as an absolutely self-authenticating experience of God. That contingency apart, one has to admit that a general appeal to the prevalence of alleged experiences of the holy or of grace is vulnerable to alternative explanations, if unsupported by rational argument or appeal to revelation, preferably both.

---

[9] M. Goulder and J. Hick, *Why Believe in God?*, London 1983.

One sees this in the aforementioned book by Goulder and Hick. Hick's unwillingness to support his case beyond appeal to experience renders it more vulnerable to Goulder's counter-arguments than it would have been had he given more weight, as Swinburne does, for example, to the rational arguments. I might add that Hick's further reluctance to support his case by appeal to a particular tradition of revelation – in the interests, of course, of a global religious ecumenism – renders his position increasingly vulnerable to Cupitt's charge that Hick's religious object has become so vague as to be indistinguishable from no object at all. For this reason, Cupitt claims that Hick is now on the side of the anti-realists – against the latter's intention, no doubt.

With these preliminaries in mind, we turn to the intellectual inadequacies of Cupitt's anti-realist faith. Cupitt's position is so extreme – his anti-realism extending not only to religion and ethics but to science, our whole life-world, indeed everything, that it is not too easy to get a purchase-hold for criticism. Moreover his anti-realism is buttressed by a reading of the whole history of philosophy as requiring this development and this development alone. In due course, this whole reading of the history of philosophy will have to be challenged; but we may begin rather more straightforwardly with the remark that any thoroughgoing anti-realist position is bound at some stage to contradict itself. For it can contain no account of that which constructs its life-worlds, its cultures, its ideals, and its religions. There is a deep unintelligibility about the creative power attributed here to humanity's myth-making capacities. In order to escape this impasse Cupitt speaks in *Life Lines* – to one's great astonishment – of 'the productive life-energy' manifesting itself in a variety of representations including the Christian ideal, which somehow, gratuitously, supervene upon the deconstruction of all essences, including the human self and will. But what on earth is this shadowy Schopenhauerian metaphysical principle – the productive life-energy – doing in Cupitt's anti-metaphysical world view? He says that there is simply nothing to be said about it except that it manifests itself in various representations. Indeed in his glossary to *Life Lines*, he says that he uses it only as a heuristic device for generating interpretations.[10] But these remarks cannot obscure the fact that at some point even the most thoroughgoing anti-metaphysics had to fall back on an ultimate metaphysical principle – in this case a totally unexplained, arbitrary and unintelligible one. As for the basic question of metaphysics – how are we to account for the world in which we find ourselves and its capacity to produce rational, personal beings such as ourselves? – this question will not go away.

In fact, of course, this question does not have to be directed at such an obscure starting-point as the 'the productive life-energy'. Anti-realism can and should be attacked from a much more straightforward starting-point, namely, its great implausibility where the given world or relatively stable natural kinds, including human beings, is concerned. It is quite a striking fact that when belief in an objective God is rejected, even the simplest and most obvious truths are liable to be rejected too. The classical admission of this in Nietzsche's famous aphorism that after the death of God truth is fiction. But the very implausibility of this attack on even the simplest truths can itself become the basis for a defence of theism. For common sense truths, tested and refined by scientific enquiry, resist such deconstruction with such compelling power that they themselves become the starting-point for an argument from truth to God. For if, without God, the most obvious truths disintegrate, then the fact that they do not disintegrate – the fact that we exist in a world whose stable, indeed rational, nature is discoverable – is suggestive of the reality of God in order to account for the existence, stability and rationality of things.

It may be pointed out in the passing that, just as a blanket theory of the inevitable immaturity of theistic religion leads to failure of discrimination where actual religious lives are concerned, so a blanket general anti-realism leads to failure of discrimination, indeed carelessness, in philosophical analysis. A striking example of this occurs in *Life Lines*, where Cupitt parodies what it is to hold that natural kinds exist with

[10] Cupitt, *Life Lines*, pp. 221ff.

the properties that they have, independent of and prior to our own experience and naming of them. He uses as an example of such a natural kind, of all things, 'a pair of scissors'.[11] Such confusion of natural and functional kinds does not inspire confidence in the accuracy of a writer's world view.

The fact that Cupitt's anti-realism in religion requires this wider, general, anti-realism constitutes a powerful argument against it. For it is not very difficult to defend philosophical realism in matters of common sense and natural science, as Michael Devitt has shown with admirable clarity in his book, *Realism and Truth*.[12] Admittedly, such a defence entails the rejection of a long tradition in Western epistemology, which interposed a private world of images or ideas between our knowing minds and the realities of which we are aware in the course of our interaction with persons and things. We have to question, indeed reject, the Kantian 'turn to the subject', which formalised this quite unjustifiable cutting off of the human mind from the world of real objects. The implausibility of the Kantian approach is once again shown up by the extremism of Kant's view. Kant treats not only the basic categories of thought, but also space and time themselves as our own modes of ordering or processing the data of sense. Things as they are in themselves disappear behind a screen of our own making. Kant was not, of course, as extreme as Cupitt. Kant thought that all human beings necessarily go on to process the data the same way in terms of the same universal conceptual scheme. Modern conceptual relativism, embraced by Cupitt, has broken this unitary system up, and speaks of different, culturally conditioned conceptual schemes, processing the data in different ways. But either way we cannot get outside our conceptual skin in order to grasp the objective nature of things. Against this whole constructivist trend, however, we need to argue that the data of sense and the concepts of the understanding, far from constituting a barrier or a screen preventing knowledge of

[11] Cupitt, *Life Lines*, p. 60.
[12] M. Devitt, *Realism and Truth*, Oxford 1984.

reality are much more plausibly to be construed as the means of direct access to the real, which products of evolution such as ourselves have best developed precisely in order to enable accurate awareness of the world of things and persons with which we have to do.

There is a problem, however, with the highly plausible defence of realism which philosophers such as Devitt offer. Such a science-based realism has some difficulty in accounting for the fact that the physical universe has evolved rational and personal beings endowed with consciousness and mind. There is a tendency to try to reduce mind to matter and to give a physicalist account of mind. Here, for once, we may agree with Cupitt in rejecting such materialism, which does not begin to do justice to the experienced character of mind and value. But having agreed with Devitt against Cupitt about the objectivity of things, we are not going to follow Cupitt in trying to solve the problem by denying objectivity as such. Much more plausible, once the objectivity of the given world is conceded, is to move in the opposite direction and take quite seriously the objectivity of mind and value. The very fact that the universe has the capacity to produce minds becomes the premise for a design argument for the existence of God.

Indeed the main intellectual failure of Cupitt's anti-realism lies in its total inability to explain anything. We have already referred to its failure to explain religious experience and, more generally, to its failure to explain truth and objectivity. We can now mention, in a little more detail, some other key features of the world that are left unexplained in Cupitt's philosophy. Once we have appreciated the case for thinking realistically about the physical universe in which we find ourselves and out of which we evolved, we can see that, while scientific explanations can plausibly be given for most changes and developments within the given system of matter or energy, operating in accordance with certain fundamental constants and laws, no explanation whatsoever is provided or could be provided by natural science for the existence of matter or energy or for why the constants and laws are precisely what they are. Most striking of all, and least of all explained by science, is the capacity of such a universe to evolve to the point where living, rational and personal beings emerge. When further we learn that the initial conditions, in the very early stages of cosmic evolution, *had* to be just what they were, if *ever* the conditions for life were to evolve, the case for postulating design is greatly enhanced. This case is further strengthened by consideration of *what* has emerged from the process of cosmic evolution. Rational, personal beings, such as ourselves, are beings endowed with freedom, openness to the future, self-transcendence, the capacity to appreciate the values of beauty, goodness and truth, and moreover to recognise the *claim* of the moral law upon us. All the features mentioned cumulatively reinforce the case for thinking that only a transcendent, creative intention, itself of surpassing value, can explain the existence and nature of the universe and what it has produced. These arguments, together with the argument from truth, support and find confirmation in, the argument from mankind's religious experience of God, to which attention has already been drawn.

It may certainly be surmised that the vague intimations of a mind and heart of love behind the whole cosmos, which both reason and experience yield, will only be clarified and systematically developed into a coherent and plausible world view, if divine revelation takes place. Only a little of the nature and intention of the Creator can be read off the existence and nature of things and persons in an ordered universe. But reason and experience lead us to expect revelation, and if God has acted to make himself known to his personal creatures then the possibility of a much more comprehensive and systematic theology arises – a theology whose intellectual scope and religious power are bound to enhance greatly the intellectual plausibility of realist faith.

Cupitt summarises the difficulties of what he calls designer realism in a short passage which bears examination:

> Its difficulties are well known. They include the logical problems of the design argument itself, the facts of evil in the world, its naively mythical anthropomorphism, and the puzzle about what the kind of disembodied person it envisages could possibly be.

Most disabling of all is its curiously weightless quality; it often seems to differ little in practice from a mere expression of innocent cosmic optimism.[13]

These controversial points are thrown out without any serious supporting arguments. Once again the disadvantage of Cupitt's extremism is revealed in its inability to make discriminations between good and bad arguments in theodicy, for example, or between a serious Christian hope for the future of God's world and a facile optimism. In fact, the logical problems of design arguments can be and are being explored and resolved in contemporary philosophy of religion with a rigour far exceeding Cupitt's impressionistic generalisations. The problem of evil too, has received searching and penetrating treatment in modern theodicy from writers such as Farrer, Hick, Plantinga and Swinburne; and the weaknesses in what in their turn can be described as the facile arguments of anti-theodicists from Hume to Mackie have been pointed out. The charge of anthropomorphism against the classical concept of God as Creator does scant justice to the Christian theological tradition which has always tried to safeguard divine transcendence and reckon with the inevitable limitations in human thought about the 'incomprehensible' deity. In fact, it is the critics of objective theism who can be observed to be thinking anthropomorphically, indeed in caricatures, of what they have rejected. Certainly the notion of infinite and incorporeal mind or spirit is not easy for us to grasp or articulate. This very notion, of course, rebuts the charge of anthropomorphism. But the idea that because we ourselves are embodied persons, personality is essentially corporeal is nothing but positivist prejudice, which no one claiming to represent the Christian theological tradition has any business to endorse. Finally, the attribution of a curiously weightless quality to designer realism ignores the way in which the recognition of design behind the world process is part and parcel of the whole tradition of Christian belief in God. There is nothing weightless about the Christian doctrine of

[13] Cupitt, *Life Lines*, p. 69.

creation and its discernment of purpose and meaning in the universe and in human life.

The intellectual inadequacy of Cupitt's position may be summarised as its total failure to account for the existence and nature of the world – and in particular for the world's finely tuned capacity to evolve rational persons, who find themselves inexorably claimed by the moral law and drawn out of themselves by the lure of beauty and love. It fails to account for humanity's religious sense the world over. And it fails utterly to account for objectivity and truth.

We turn to the ethical inadequacy of Cupitt's anti-realist faith. This may be pin-pointed by drawing attention to the Prometheanism of his conviction that humanity has it in itself to create or invent value. Keith Ward has acknowledged the ethically proper, indeed essential, senses in which men and women are morally autonomous beings.[14] They are free and responsible, and must acknowledge and interiorise for themselves the claims of the moral law. But Cupitt has pushed the notion of ethical autonomy to quite untenable extremes. Only if men and women create their own realms of value are they autonomous moral beings in his sense. But this position, like all forms of anti-realism, self-destructs. It undermines and destroys the very nature of value which of its essence lays a claim upon the mind and heart of the moral agent. It is indeed up to us to decide whether we will acknowledge and respond to the needs of the neighbour in distress, but in no way do we ourselves create that obligation. Respect for human rights is not an optional stance for us to adopt. Such a view reduces morality, as it does religion, to a purely human product – an item on the supermarket shelf.

Cupitt replies to the charge of Prometheanism (as brought by Rowan Williams, for example, in a powerful article)[15] in his book *Life Lines*.[16] The religious voluntarist, he declares, in affirming the Christian ideal against the background of a Nietzschean void, is not like the atheist existentialist,

[14] J. K. S. Ward, *Holding Fast to God*, London 1982.
[15] R. Williams, 'Religious Realism: On not Quite Agreeing with Don Cupitt', *Modern Theology*, Vol. 1, No. 1, October 1984, pp. 3–24.
[16] Cupitt, *Life Lines*, p. 130.

overcoming nothingness by an act of Promethean self-affir-
mation. On the contrary, the self too is dissolved. Christianity
is rather a matter of the 'productive life-energy's' inexplicable
resurgence. Love appears out of nothing as pure gift. It is
entirely gratuitous. There is an extraordinary effort here to
avoid ascribing the power of *agape* either to God or to the
human self. I have already commented on Cupitt's wilful
obscurantism in introducing the notion of the 'productive life-
energy'. If he really means this as no more than a heuristic
device, we are barred from taking it as a veiled reference,
despite himself, to the creative Spirit of God. But if this
metaphysical route is barred, then there is no alternative to
treating the affirmation of Christian love as a purely human
phenomenon or possibility. It may not be an act of individual
will, but it is a purely human creation all the same. But the
point of the Prometheus legend, like that of all powerful
myths, is not restricted to the portrayal of an individual's
rebellion and taking to himself the prerogatives of God. On
the contrary, the figure of Prometheus symbolises *humankind*'s
arrogation of divine prerogatives. Cupitt's purely human
Christianity is just as open to the charge of Prometheanism as
is atheistic existentialism.

This is the point at which the tables must be turned on
Cupitt's remark that 'realism always has an itch of egoism
about it'. On the contrary, the ethical significance of theological realism lies in the way in which it sees our own true
good as consisting precisely in being drawn out of ourselves,
away from our fantasies and self-projections, into relation to
the Love that made us. We are, as Bonhoeffer insisted, to be
conformed to the reality of God in Christ. In face of that
reality our illusions fall away and our self-assertion is overcome. The notion that Bonhoeffer, of all people, is Cupitt's
secret ally, is a crowning instance of the topsy-turvy way in
which the very opposite of Cupitt's position gets claimed as
his own. The ethical profundity of Bonhoeffer's writings,
rather, lies precisely in his insight into the identity of the ideal
and the real in *Christ*, and the consequent conformity to Christ
required of us, his disciples. This theological realism is the
very reverse of egoistic. Christian self-noughting, Christian

altruism, is not an aimless, arbitrary deconstruction of the self. It is a redirection, a refocusing of the self and the community on a power, a Spirit, a love, not ourselves, that makes for righteousness – to fill out Matthew Arnold's famous phrase with the theological content that it still requires for intelligibility.

For Christian ethics teaches us that men and women, whether as individuals or as a community, do not have it in themselves either to invent or to realise the good. A further ethical inadequacy of Cupitt's position, therefore, lies in its failure to do justice to people's need for help, for resources from beyond, if they are to be enabled to change and to love altruistically. This is, of course, the ethical aspect of people's need for grace, to which reference was made above when the religious inadequacy of Cupitt's position was under discussion. What is now being stressed is the ethical appropriateness, indeed, ultimately speaking, the ethical necessity of recognition of dependence on God as constitutive both of virtue and of the common good.

The ethical insecurity of Cupitt's view is manifested in his location of all values on the surface of things, a range of merely human possibilities to be embraced at will. Worse than this, the affirmation of complete relativity – and hence the 'affirmation of everything'[17] – leads quite explicitly to an Eastern dissolution and elimination of all objective distinctions whatsoever. But if that is seriously meant, then the distinction between good and evil disappears as well, and we are left with an endless blissful 'flux of experience', whose amoral consequences were most powerfully brought out by R. C. Zaehner.[18] Such an overt transcendence of good and evil is not to be attributed to Cupitt himself. He still commends the virtue of disinterested love. But without metaphysical depth or objective support in the nature of things this virtue is as fragile and as insecure as anything could be.

To sum up the ethical inadequacies of Cupitt's position: it is implausibly Promethean in treating humanity as the

[17] Cupitt, *Life Lines*, p. 188.
[18] R. C. Zaehner, *Our Savage God*, London 1974.

inventor of right and wrong, and at the same time it is wilfully blind to men and women's need for resources of transformation and sanctification from beyond. It is also in danger of total collapse, if ethical distinctions themselves are part only of the surface of things, to be dissolved in the flux of experience.

Having surveyed the religious, intellectual and ethical inadequacies of Cupitt's 'Christian Buddhism', we may conclude with some reflections on the different ways in which the history of philosophy can be read. It is, of course, possible to trace the collapse of metaphysical realism through Hume and Kant to Schopenhauer and Nietzsche, and then to interpret twentieth-century philosophy, particularly in the light of Wittgenstein and Heidegger, as drawing the consequences of this collapse and offering instead a range of purely human options – nihilism, existentialism, Marxism, deconstructionism, and, among them, an anti-realist, expressivist, version of Christianity. It is clear that, for Cupitt, there is no alternative to this way of reading the history of philosophy. But in fact there are many different ways of reading the history of philosophy, and many different possibilities for a recovery of metaphysics today, of which Process Philosophy is only one. For the steps in the story chronicled by Cupitt may well have included some major false steps, which have led philosophers further and further into error, until the implausibility or absurdity of the consequences forces us to re-examine the whole story from way back in the sequence. Kant's transcendental idealism may serve as an example. As argued above, its constructivist, relativist, consequences have now led to such extreme forms of anti-realism that common sense and working science alike rebel, and force us to reconstruct a more objective conception of the universe in which we find ourselves. The trouble began much earlier than Kant, of course. It is widely recognised today how damaging to understanding of the nature of things was Descartes' peculiarly solipsistic project of enquiry or Locke's assumption that 'ideas' were the immediate objects of experience. None of the great philosophers whom I have just mentioned were atheists; but, for all that, much of the story traced by Cupitt concerns their increasingly atheistic successors' determination to draw out the full consequences of a consistent atheism. Bishop Berkeley foresaw that this would be so, and tried to stem the tide – in quite the wrong way, of course – by dispensing with matter altogether. On such a premise, Berkeley quite plausibly required God to account for the order of our ideal world. Entirely different reasons for postulating God have been advanced in this chapter. We have claimed that theism guarantees reality, objectivity and truth, in both the material and the spiritual spheres. What strikes one as extraordinary in Cupitt's position is the way in which he unquestioningly embraces atheist philosophy and translates the heart of Christianity into a completely atheistic form. One has to admit that this is something of a tour de force. But the Christian philosopher really has no business to be holding on to the coat-tails of atheism, as it has expressed itself since Nietzsche in ever more bizarre and self-destructive philosophical forms. As Alvin Plantinga has argued,[19] Christian philosophy has its own agenda and has a right to its own perspectives. From its own theistic standpoint it must question the presuppositions and shibboleths of post-Enlightenment thought. It must attack the implausible subjectivist epistemology characteristic of that philosophy and it must attack the reductionist scientism which accompanied it. At the same time, Christian philosophy must expose the manifest contradiction between these two pervasive aspects of post-Enlightenment philosophy. For either the turn to the subject renders modern science incomprehensible or else modern science renders the human subject incomprehensible. The task of Christian philosophy is to show that only theism makes sense of both. With such rational support we can then take seriously again the claims of divine revelation and the testimony of religious experience to the reality of God.[20]

---

[19] A. Plantinga, 'Advice to Christian Philosophers', *Faith and Philosophy*, Vo.l. 1, No. 3, 1984, pp. 253–71.

[20] I have endeavoured to make out the case against Don Cupitt's views and for objective theism in B. L. Hebblethwaite, *The Ocean of Truth*, Cambridge 1988.

9

⟨ornament⟩

John Hick and the question of truth in religion

John Hick's writings on the philosophy of religion reveal an increasing tension between his commitment to critical realism regarding the cognitive fact-asserting nature of religious language on the one hand and the key devices which he employs in order to work out and defend a philosophy of religious pluralism on the other. In this chapter we shall argue that it is the Kantian element in Hick's epistemology that both enables him to hold these two basic positions together at one and the same time, notwithstanding the tension, and also accounts for the threat which Hick's religious pluralism now poses to his critical realism.

Hick's commitment to critical realism is evident from his inaugural lecture at Birmingham in 1967[1] to his contribution to the Realism/Anti-Realism Conference in Claremont in 1988.[2] These two pieces reflect decades of polemic against the so-called 'Wittgensteinian fideism' of D. Z. Phillips, as well as against earlier 'non-cognitivists', such as A. J. Ayer, R. B. Braithwaite and J. H. Randall. Hick has, of course, been more concerned with religiously sympathetic figures such as Braithwaite, Randall and Phillips (and, latterly, Don Cupitt) than with the anti-religious logical positivists such as Ayer. And indeed it is the former who represent the greater threat to Christian self-understanding; for they challenge a cognitive or realist conception of the faith not from outside but from

[1] J. H. Hick, *God and the Universe of Faiths*, London 1973, ch. 1.
[2] Published in J. Runzo (ed.), *Is God Real?*, London 1993.

within. This issue – whether or not Christian God-talk is referential, conveying truth about transcendent matters of ultimate concern – was spoken of by Hick in 1967 as 'theology's central problem',[3] and it has continued to pre-occupy him to the present day. Hick still holds that religion, whatever else it is, is 'fact-asserting', including, that is, truth-claims in the sense of putative articulations of how things really or ultimately are. Thus, in the Claremont paper, he argues that the cosmic optimism of the great world faiths depends upon a realist interpretation of their language. Only if it is *true* that the world has a transcendent meaning and a future goal that will indeed be realised in the end, have they any genuine hope to extend to suffering humanity.

That this commitment to critical realism remains, despite Hick's more recent espousal and defence of a philosophy of religious pluralism is clear from the way in which this pluralism is expressed. Each major 'post-Axial'[4] world faith constitutes a possible salvific path from self-centredness to Reality-centredness.[5] The vehicle of each such path is religious experience; but it is the testimony of (nearly) all forms of religious experience that they are experience *of* transcendent, ultimate, Reality – albeit under various guises. Salvific experience, therefore, in its many forms, points to a trans-cendent Real as its source and goal.[6] There are thus implicit truth claims about the transcendent embedded in (nearly) all the practical life-transforming and life-reorienting religious traditions in the post-Axial history of humankind.

But if an underlying cognitive realism is retained through-out the corpus of his writings, Hick's understanding of the truth-content of such implicit claims has undergone a sea-change. Whereas in early books the cognitive aspect of religious experience was articulated in the language of biblical

[3] Hick, *God and the Universe of Faiths*, loc. cit.
[4] This phrase goes back to Karl Jaspers. It refers to the turning point in the history of religions when the great world faiths emerged. See J. H. Hick, *An Interpretation of Religion*, London 1989, pp. 29ff.
[5] J. H. Hick, *Problems of Religious Pluralism*, London 1985, p. 44.
[6] Hick, *An Interpretation of Religion*, ch. 11.

faith in a personal God revealed in Christ,[7] in later writings Hick speaks of an Ultimate, or a Real, manifested now in the personal representations of the theistic faiths, now in the impersonal representations of Theravada Buddhism or monistic Vedantic Hinduism.[8] What enables continuity in Hick's overall view, despite this pretty drastic change, is a basically Kantian epistemology concerning both the nature of truth and human access to truth.

As is well known, for Hick, religious truth is grasped, in faith, through a particular way of interpreting experience.[9] Faith is defined as the interpretative element within religious experience. This involves the application to the religious case of a more general epistemology of interpretation. All experience is experiencing-as. Raw experience is indefinite or ambiguous until interpreted as significant in some specific way. This occurs at every level of our experience – natural, moral and religious. Even at the level of our experience of the natural world, the mind is active in applying a range of concepts to what is given, so that we construe ourselves as living in a material world of interacting objects. The ambiguity, at this level, is minimal. Ordinary everyday experience presupposes a basic realist interpretation, even though our everyday world-view involves a selection of practically-relevant features of the given. Moral experience is less immediate. It involves seeing the sphere of interpersonal life as imposing certain demands and obligations upon us. It is quite possible to miss or turn a blind eye to such significance. Religious experience, in its Christian mode, involves experiencing the whole world as God's creation and the sphere of God's providence. Our whole lives become a response to the immanent presence of this transcendent Spirit, and we look, in faith, for an eschatological consummation, beyond death, when all ambiguity will be resolved. For ambiguity is at its greatest in the case of religious experience. Our whole world and our own lives *can* be experienced naturalistically. On

---

[7] Hick, *God and the Universe of Faiths*, ch. 3.
[8] Hick, *An Interpretation of Religion*, chs. 15 and 16.
[9] J. H. Hick, *Faith and Knowledge*, 2nd edn., Ithaca 1989, ch. 5.

Hick's view, this would be a systematic error, but it is quite rational. Equally rational is the decision of faith, whereby the religious interpretation is allowed to structure our whole life-world. Such a faith perspective, Hick believes, is true and will be confirmed as true in the end.

The Kantian element in all this is the stress on the contribution of the knowing mind to the interpretation of experience as naturally, morally, or religiously significant. This contribution is not arbitrary. There are less and more appropriate ways of so structuring our experience as to gain access to reality; but since at each level reality is apprehended through our own interpretative concepts, we only know it as it appears to creatures endowed with sensible, moral, and spiritual faculties such as ours. Kant is not in fact mentioned in Hick's earlier writings on 'experiencing-as', except in respect of our experience of a categorical moral demand; but that Hick's whole epistemology is fundamentally Kantian is confirmed by the Gifford Lectures, where Kant's seminal distinction between noumenon and phenomenon, between the thing in itself and how it appears to beings such as ourselves, is explicitly transferred from the basic case of our knowledge of our perceived environment to the more controversial case of the epistemology of religion.[10]

By this time, of course, the religious interpretation is not restricted to its Christian mode. There is an intriguing parallel with the story of post-Kantain general epistemology here. For Kant the world appears to beings endowed with faculties of sense and understanding such as ours in only one shared way. Even though we do not have access to the world as it is in itself, the world as it appears, the phenomenol world, is a uniform, public world that we all experience similarly and that Newtonian science explores and describes systematically. Post-Kantian philosophy has lost this confidence. The possibility of many different, perhaps systematically incommensurable, ways of interpreting the data of experience have been explored by writers such as Quine.[11] Hick now sees a comparable plurality

---

[10] Hick, *An Interpretation of Religion*, pp. 240ff.
[11] W. V. Quine, *Ontological Relativity and Other Essays*, New York 1969.

in ways of interpreting the world religiously. Whereas in the early writings, religious faith was spoken of solely in Christian terms – as experience of a personal God of creation, providence, and eventual redemption – now, in the more recent writings, this is seen as only one of a range of phenomenal representations of the ultimate noumenal reality that are not only possible but actual in the history of religions. Hick's so-called 'Copernican revolution', like Kant's, transfers much of what used, pre-critically (or even critically, in Hick's case) to be ascribed to the object of religious experience to one way in which that unknown noumenal object appears to those of us nurtured in a particular religious tradition. Hick now employs a neutral term, 'the Real', for the ultimate transcendent, noumenal, religious object, and relocates the God of Judaeo-Christian theism among the various 'personae' of the Real, that is, the set of ways in which, for certain traditions, notably those of Semitic origin, but also for devotional Hinduism and other Eastern and African faiths, the Real is represented as a divine Thou, evocative of worship, and sustaining human beings in a variety òf life-transforming ways. In these personal modes, the spiritual resources of the transcendent are experienced as grace and love. But there are other traditions, equally resourceful in spiritual life-transforming power, which represent the Real, phenomenally, through various 'impersonae' – that is, interpretations of the Real as a non-personal Absolute, as Brahman in Vedantic Hinduism, for example, or Nirvana or Sunyata in the various Buddhist schools.[12] In these traditions of interpretation, union with the absolute yields peace, bliss and unlimited compassion. The ethical and salvific effectiveness of all these ways of religiously 'experiencing-as' forbids our attempting to 'grade' them from some allegedly neutral standpoint.[13]

Let us now ask how the question of truth in religion fares in this newer pluralistic context. Previously, as we have seen, it was the concepts supplied by the Christian tradition that enabled Hick to interpret his religious experience, cognitively,

---

[12] Hick, *An Interpretation of Religion*, ch. 16.
[13] Hick, *Problems of Religious Pluralism*, ch. 5.

as experience of an ultimate, personal, source of grace and love, to be encountered unambiguously, though still mediated through the (now risen) Christ, in the eschaton. These were basic religious truths, both disclosed in and evocative of Christian salvific experience. Despite the interpretative processing involved, Christian faith gave cognitive access to the noumenally real as actually being personal and gracious. But now, in the pluralist context, nearly all these alleged truths are transferred to the phenomenal level. They cease to be true of ultimate reality as it is in itself. One might still say that they remain true of that reality *as it appears* in one of its personalist manifestations. But Hick himself is more inclined to speak of them now as *myths*, expressive of religiously appropriate attitudes, namely attitudes conducive to ethical and spiritual transformation, from self-centredness to Reality-centredness.

We encounter this shift regarding the truth-content of religious beliefs at what might be termed its half-way stage in the book *Truth and Dialogue*,[14] which came out of a 1970 conference in Birmingham on the apparently conflicting truth-claims of the world religions. The conference was dominated by the contribution of Wilfred Cantwell Smith and reactions to it. For Cantwell Smith, religious truth is not propositional, cognitive, or fact-asserting, but rather personal – a life-transforming quality of sincerity and commitment – as persons inwardly appropriate their faith's spiritual power and vision. In his own essay in this book, Hick endorses the practical orientation of Cantwell Smith's view, but points out that a religion can only become true in the latter's existential, personalistic sense if it is already true in a more universal and objective sense. Neither Christianity nor Islam could become true if there were no God. Hick, therefore, retains his critical realistic account, even when endorsing the practical, personalist, approach. (It is clear that the same must in fact be said of Cantwell Smith himself, as later work has shown).[15] The problem of conflicting truth claims therefore

[14] J. H. Hick (ed.), *Truth and Dialogue*, London 1974.
[15] W. Cantwell Smith, *Toward a World Theology*, London 1981.

remains. Hick goes on to consider the hypothesis that all the great religions are in contact with the same ultimate divine reality, but that their differing experiences of that reality, shaped over centuries in different historical and cultural contexts, have received different conceptualisations in their respective theologies. It is this basically Kantian distinction between experience and interpretation that enables Hick to graft his emerging pluralism on to his long-standing critical realism. At this stage the suggestion is of complementary rather than of rival truths.[16] Hick is optimistic here about the possibility of convergence and the discovery of common ground, even between the personal and non-personal experiences of what he still calls the divine. At the doctrinal level, however, he is already resorting to the language of myth, as one way of dealing with a disputed doctrine such as that of reincarnation.

'Myth' becomes an increasingly important category in Hick's writings during the 1970s and 80s, most notably and notoriously in connection with *The Myth of God Incarnate*.[17] There 'myth' is defined as 'a story which is told but which is not literally true, or an idea or image which is applied to someone or something but which does not literally apply, but which invites a particular attitude in its hearers',[18] and it is used particularly of the Incarnation which must, indeed, be 'demythologised', if the pluralistic hypothesis is to be sustained. This definition of myth, not surprisingly, has been attacked as being purely subjectivist and expressivist; but, of course, that does not do justice to Hick's intention. The 'Myth' of God incarnate may express an attitude to Jesus, but the attitude in question is still one of reverence for and commitment to one who has enabled and whose memory still sustains the Christian form of salvific encounter with God. So there are still underlying truth claims about God involved in mythical talk about Jesus. The situation is very similar to that of Hick's own reply to Cantwell Smith.

---

[16] Hick, *Truth and Dialogue*, p. 152.
[17] J. H. Hick (ed.), *The Myth of God Incarnate*, London 1977.
[18] Hick, *The Myth of God Incarnate*, p. 178.

In subsequent writings, this notion of the mythological is greatly extended. Indeed, in the Gifford Lectures, it is suggested that talk of God (as of Nirvana) functions mythologically *vis-à-vis* the transcendent Real.[19] Hick is clearer now about the implicit reference to the Real – we might call this the residual truth claim in the pluralist hypothesis – that underlies the attitudinal definition of myth. Myths express appropriate attitude and responses that enable salvific re-alignments with the Real. A certain residual tension remains, however, between what Hick says at this point about the mythological function of religious language and what he says at the end of the book when when explicitly addressing the problem of conflicting truth claims. In the penultimate chapter it seems that all the doctrines of all the religions refer at the phenomenal level only to personae or impersonae of the Real. In so far as they refer beyond the phenomenal to the noumenal Real, they function mythologically. But in the final chapter, the category of myth appears to be restricted to specific narratives like those of creation, incarnation, or eternal life, while the primary underlying affirmations may yet be discovered to be complementary.[20] It must be said that the bulk of the Gifford Lectures favours the former rather than the latter view. The final chapter seems to revert to what was called the half-way stage where complementarity still remains a possibility. The main thrust of the Gifford Lectures lies in the direction of extending the category of myth to cover all aspects of phenomenal manifestations of the Real. Personae and impersonae alike are phenomenal, and everything we say about them is therefore mythological *vis-à-vis* the Real. In other words, Hick has become less optimistic about cognitive complementarity, and tends to fall back on comparable salvific efficacy.

This means that the ultimate referent of religious language – the noumenal Real, lying behind all phenomenal representations – becomes more and more vague and unknown as Hicks's Copernican revolution gets further developed. As

[19] Hick, *An Interpretation of Religion*, p. 351.
[20] Hick, *An Interpretation of Religion*, p. 374.

with Kant's noumenon, virtually nothing can be said about it. We have no cognitive access to it. Only a practical faith – the aforementioned salvific transformation from self-centredness – bears witness to the unknown Real responsible for such effects in all the different (indeed incommensurable) forms of spiritual life.

But it may well be asked whether it is necessary to retain such a vague transcendent reference point? Just as post-Kantian phenomenalists and constructivists accept Kant's analysis of the contribution of the knowing mind to what it knows but drop all reference to an inaccessible noumenon lying behind the phenomena, so Don Cupitt now suggests that Hick's religious 'personae' and 'impersonae' can be appropriated as human social constructs without the postulation of a transcendent Real behind them. They may still be spiritually effective in the lives of different communities of faith even if there is no ultimate object of faith at all. On Cupitt's view, Hick's ever-receding noumenal object has become so vague as to be entirely redundant. It is in this sense that the Kantian element in Hick's epistemology, developed and deployed in defence of religious pluralism, has become a threat to his critical realism. And, of course, if the single noumenal Real is dropped, the variety of salvific life-ways becomes un-problematic.

It is worth pondering the reasons why Hick wishes, against Cupitt and all non-cognitivists, to retain a transcendent noumenal Real, even though we have no access to it as it is in itself. There is no doubt that Hick believes that religious myths do express experiences and attitudes that are not self-supporting. In the context of both personalist and impersonalist faiths they are responses to, evoked by, and sustained in relation to something from beyond both the natural and the human worlds. Intriguingly, Hick's well-known notion of eschatological verification still provides the litmus test of the fact-asserting nature of religious language. For it is an implication of all the great faiths that human beings are not snuffed out at death but caught up into a further purifying process which will demonstrate, less and less ambiguously, that their beliefs about an ultimate resource of spiritual transformation were true. Once again there has been a pretty drastic change in Hick's assessment of the details of this eschatological hope. No single heavenly scenario will now perform this role. The ultimate will continue to be manifested, albeit less ambiguously, in a variety of phenomenal forms - but the fact that this process continues beyond death will verify the critically realistic claim that the personae and impersonae of the Real are indeed of the Real and not purely human constructions. For purely human constructions are bound to end for all of us at death.

A footnote in the Gifford Lectures bears this out.[21] In his book, *Theology and Religious Pluralism*,[22] Gavin D'Costa had argued that eschatological verification would require the prediction of a single ultimate future state, which would thus refute the pluralistic hypothesis. Hick replies that 'the cosmic optimism of post-axial religion expects a limitlessly good fulfilment of the project of human existence. But this fulfilment could take many forms . . .' So even in respect of eschatological verification our predictions, and perhaps our post-mortem experience themselves, retain the character of mythical representations. The only residual truth claims in the cognitively realist sense is that there will be some such limitless good fulfilment beyond death.

It is worth attempting to list the residual, underlying, noumenal, truth claims, to which Hick remains committed, despite the increasing weight he places on different phenomenal manifestations in the religions of the world. They are:

1. There is an ultimate transcendent Reality, to which all human religions, in their very different modes, are historically and culturally shaped responses.
2. Salvific religious experience, leading to transformation from self-centredness to Reality-centredness, is not a purely human possibility. Religion, in all its different forms, involves spiritual resources from beyond.
3. Human life will be extended, beyond death, towards some form of perfected consummation in the end.

[21] Hick, *An Interpretation of Religion*, p. 361.
[22] G. D'Costa, *Theology and Religious Pluralism*, Oxford 1986.

It is difficult to see that there are any further assertions of transcendent fact which Hick could now endorse in the light of his pluralistic hypothesis. All other religious assertions function mythologically, expressing attitudes evoked either by historical figures or merely phenomenal representations.

Two questions may be posed regarding Hick's now minimal critical realism. In the first place, can these three residual truth claims resist the threat of collapse into redundancy in the light of purely expressivistic, constructivist, alternatives? And, secondly, can religious believers be expected to accept that these three residual truth claims represent the cognitive heart of their traditions' central doctrines? The first question is a question for philosophers of religion, the second for the respective members of each community of faith.

Both questions seem to call for answers in the negative. It is highly dubious that religious experience alone can be thought to carry the weight of sustaining such minimal and vague claims concerning the transcendent. Even if it is conceded that all the world faiths may be construed in this way, that they *must* be construed seems very implausible in the light of the alternative accounts (by no means all hostile or reductive in any pejorative sense) that are now available. The second question can only be answered from within a particular faith community; but it seems that Buddhists as well as Christians, Hindus as well as Muslims, will resist the relegation of their most characteristic doctrines to the level of appearance, functioning only mythologically *vis-à-vis* the Real.

Any challenge to Hick from the realist side of this debate must go right back to the Kantian epistemology which has allowed this gradual process of erosion towards the affirmation of an increasingly minimal set of truth claims about the transcendent, in the interests of the pluralistic hypothesis. Kant greatly overestimated the contribution of the knowing mind to how what is known appears. This is most obviously true of space and time, which must surely be admitted to be relational dimensions of the world as it is discovered to be in itself – and to have been long before human minds evolved. But it is also true of the categories and concepts in terms of which we process the data of sense and understand ourselves and our world. Our basic categories are required by and evoked by the very nature of what we encounter all the time, and our concepts, though partial and selective, are likewise determined by the given nature of things as we discover them to be. Similarly our moral experience is of objective demands and claims that impose themselves upon us in the dictates of conscience, irrespective of and sometimes despite social conditioning. And if we admit the force of reason and revelation as well as that of experience in the sphere of religion, we will, at least in the context of the religions of Semitic origin, find ourselves constrained to affirm that ultimate reality is personal and not impersonal, graciously active and not inert, and to hope realistically for a consummation beyond death that will take the form of a perfected communion of love and not absorption into a featureless Absolute. Christians will go further than this in claiming that God's personality and love have been definitively revealed in the Incarnation, whose truth they therefore maintain.

The upshot of this discussion is that, when we have firmly rejected, as we must, Kantian epistemology in all its forms, we will find ourselves able to make many more discriminating truth claims in religion than Hick's pluralistic hypothesis can allow. Among them will be a different hypothesis concerning the relation between the truths contained in the Christian tradition and truths contained in other religions.[23]

---

[23] For further reflections on these issues, see G. D'Costa (ed.), *Christian Uniqueness Reconsidered*, Maryknoll, NY 1990.

10

The problem of evil as a practical problem

All human beings, whether they are religious or not, find themselves confronted by the problem of suffering and evil. We live in a world where we are all prone to sickness, accidental mutilation, natural disaster, bereavement and untimely death. And we are all potential or actual victims of human wickedness (that of other people or our own) in the varied forms of war, injustice, cruelty, greed or hate. These are the facts which form the starting point of our reflections in these last three chapters. They are deliberately characterised, to start with, in non-religious terms. We shall eventually have much to say about Buddhist, Christian and Hindu ways of regarding these facts and about the various religious responses to them; but, for our starting point, we say nothing of *dukkha*, 'sin' or *maya*. We simply point to the empirical facts of pain and agony, cruelty and violence.

We live at a time in history, when for some at least of the earth's inhabitants, some of these problems have been eased and tamed to an unprecedented degree. But it has to be admitted that human success in overcoming them is slow, limited and very unevenly distributed. Moreover, any success in the overcoming of evil is counterbalanced in our time by the vast increase in global communications which present us every day of our lives with countless stories of horror and tragedy from all over the world as we open our newspapers or switch on the television. The result is that despite our limited success in making the world a better place, we are more conscious than ever before of the extent and depth of the world's pain. It is no wonder then that very many people in the modern world find it hard to retain any confidence in the basic goodness of human existence as it manifests itself so precariously in vitality, happiness, creativity, spirituality and love.

Religious minds confront the problem of evil in an enormous variety of ways. Our treatment in these chapters is bound to be selective. For one thing, treatment is restricted here to the three religions, or families of religions, which go by the names of Buddhism, Christianity and Hinduism. And as the titles of these three chapters show, our intention is to concentrate on those *practical* responses to suffering and evil that stem from or are fostered by the three religions just named. Moreover, relatively little space will be given to the kind of descriptive work which characterises the comparative study or phenomenology of religion. Our viewpoint, rather, is that of the philosophy of religion and ethics. We are interested primarily in identifying and evaluating not only the differences and internal developments, but also the interactions and potentialities of these religions' practical responses to the problem of evil.

Our choice of these three faiths inevitably leads us to concentrate attention on India, where Hinduism, Buddhism and Christianity – to say nothing of Islam – have been in such creative tension and interaction for so long. And while there are other parts of the world where the problem of evil is even more starkly posed – one thinks of Bosnia and the Sudan – it will doubtless be agreed that India has more than its fair share of evils to contend with, in the forms of poverty and natural disasters, and of injustice and communal violence.

Our intention to concentrate on *practical* responses to the problem of evil should not obscure the fact that belief and practice are inextricably linked, and a central aim, especially of the present chapter, is to look at the mutual implications of belief and practice in the three religious traditions which we have chosen to consider. It is often held that men and women of religion should ignore their differences of belief and stick to practical co-operation towards the elimination of suffering. But, except in very obvious cases like the rescuing of a drowning man or organising relief work after an earthquake, our commitment to practical action towards the overcoming of evil will reflect and be conditioned by our understanding of the world and of human life within it. It will be affected too, by what we believe are the resources available to men and women for coping with suffering and evil, and for transforming the conditions that make for suffering and evil. Moreover, partly through the interaction of religions and partly through the internal development of each religion in face of the secular movements of our time, religious approaches to the problem of evil are in process of very rapid change. It is impossible to assess the potentiality of the religions for making some contribution towards the overcoming of evil by examining their scriptures and traditions alone.

These issues of belief and practice, including this problem of religion and change as faiths develop and interact with each other and with secular pressures, will form the topic of this present chapter. The next, pursuing the theme of practical response, will endeavour to examine the tension between the more individualist and the more collectivist emphases in religious responses to the problem of evil. There we shall be asking how far the religions, in themselves or through interaction of co-operation, can hope to produce and foster a viable social ethic for the modern world. Then, in the final chapter, we will explore more closely the actual religious resources claimed to be available to humanity for the overcoming of evil and especially of social evil, and we will press the question how far these religious resources may be expected to contribute to the solution of specific problem areas, such as those of ecological disaster, sexism, war, world poverty and social injustice generally.

Our main concern in these chapters is with social evils which could, in theory, be overcome here on earth in the historical future. But the topic was introduced in broader terms, with reference not only to moral and social evils such as cruelty, injustice and war, but also to natural evils, such as the suffering brought about by natural disaster, sickness and death. Some evils, world poverty, for example, straddle this division, being partly due to natural shortages of the necessities of life and partly due to their unfair distribution. There are four reasons why we need to keep this broader problem of evil in mind – that is the problem of natural evil or suffering as well as that of moral and social evil or wickedness. In the first place our concentration on the practical problem of overcoming evil should not get too far detached from the theoretical problem of understanding why there is so much evil, natural as well as moral, in the world. In the second place, we have to remember that the religions differ very greatly over where they see the main problem of evil to lie. Buddhism, for example, locates the problem in an all-pervasive suffering that characterises all sentient life in this world. Thirdly, even if we concentrate on the overcoming of moral and social evil in human life, this includes the way in which we respond to the ravages of natural evil and the urgency with which we tackle the problems of malnutrition, sickness and natural disaster. And fourthly, we should not forget that some religions, certainly Christianity, but also the more eschatological forms of Buddhism and devotional Hinduism, speak of the ultimate overcoming of all natural as well as moral and social evil, of a time when there will be no more pain, no more crying, no more death. For these reasons, our starting-point, our initial picture of the evils that afflict humanity, needs to be as broad as possible, including natural as well as moral and social evil.

One further preliminary point must be made. No one can study the problem of evil in the context of religion without consideration of the ambiguity of the phenomenon of religion in the history of the world. Reflection on religious resources for the overcoming of evil should not blind us to the fact that a large number of people hold religion to be responsible for many of the world's ills. The catalogue of evils perpetrated in the name of religion is very long and although many practices such as the burning of so-called witches at the stake or of widows on their husbands' funeral pyres are almost entirely things of the past and resolutely condemned within the religious traditions that once encouraged them, we have only to think of contemporary situations of inter-communal violence, whether in Northern Ireland, the Balkans or Sri

Lanka, to realise the continuing force of the moral repudiation of religion as a divisive factor rather than a unitive and healing one. Again, it might well be pointed out that most of the forward-looking social and political movements which hold out some promise of ameliorating the human condition on earth are thoroughly secular in inspiration. One thinks in this connection not only of Marxism (notwithstanding its recent fall from favour in eastern Europe and the former Soviet Union), but also of democratic socialism too. In subsequent chapters we will have something to say about the relation between socialism and the three religions with which we are concerned. For the moment, we simply note the existence of powerful modern ideologies, devoted to the overcoming of evil, which ignore or repudiate religion as an enemy rather than a friend.

Of course, it can be argued that modern secular ideologies, such as Marxism, socialism, humanism (and even capitalism, if Max Weber is to be believed) are not in fact of secular inspiration but are rather products of a religious and indeed Judaeo-Christian background. There are complex historical issues at stake here, but whatever the origin of these movements may be, they have certainly become independent secular voices, challenging the competence of religion to contribute anything of more than marginal value towards the overcoming of evil. Of course, these voices are themselves widely challenged. Indeed, it will be suggested here that secular resources alone are even less likely to overcome the world's ills that are those of the religions, and that, even if the religions need the stimulus of secular ideologies to awaken them to their full potential, the spiritual dimension is an essential element in any lasting hope for the overcoming of evil.

Let us now turn to the question of the relation between theory and practice, not only in a religious but in any comprehensive approach to the overcoming of evil. Our reflections on this matter begin with a reference to A. C. Danto's *Mysticism and Morality*,[1] in which the author shows how

---

[1] A. C. Danto, *Mysticism and Morality*, New York 1972.

closely integrated with overall *beliefs* about the nature of the
world are the moral policies of action recommended and
fostered, especially in the religions of the world. As Danto
observes, the appropriateness and persuasiveness of these
moral policies depend to a considerable extent on the truth
or falsity of the beliefs and world views in which they are
embedded. Of course, there is a complication here, perhaps
not sufficiently recognised by Danto, namely, the far from
straightforward nature of the question of the truth or falsity
of religious beliefs. Religious systems cannot easily be
categorised as true or false. This is not only a consequence of
their complexity, so that a particular religious tradition may
contain many truths and many falsehoods at the same time,
but also a consequence of the fact that a deeper, all-embracing
truth may lie behind the superficial apparent falsehoods
within a religion or apparent incompatibilities between
religions. Nevertheless, the fact remains that, for example, the
Buddhist *dharma* retains its plausibility as a policy of right
action just so far as the Buddha's diagnosis of the nature of
the world and of the human condition is judged to be true.

This chapter began by stressing, in as uncontroversial and
empirical a way as possible, the common evils and sufferings
to which humankind is subject the world over. But it has now
to be acknowledged that the way in which men and women
actually see and experience the problem of evil depends very
much on their basic beliefs. For theists it is often primarily a
problem for the understanding. How can God permit such
horrors in his world? The nature and the extent of suffering
and wickedness make people doubt the power or the goodness
of God. But not all theists are struck by the problem in the
same way. Some theists – many Jews and most Muslims, for
example – tend to think it religiously improper to press such
moral objections to belief in a creator God. Others – many
Hindus, for example – do not feel the presence of evil and
suffering as a moral objection to belief in God; for God is not
thought of in such heavily moral terms. Even where the
problem is felt as a moral difficulty for belief in God, it is not
always felt so in the same way. For some theists, the extent of
physical suffering through natural disaster represents the

heart of the problem. For others, it is the radical nature of human wickedness that is harder to understand. What is at stake here are not only the different conceptions of God that are fostered and sustained in the theistic religions. There is also the question of how the world and humankind are understood both in themselves and in relation to God. A doctrine of the world being created out of nothing reinforces the problem of evil as a problem for the understanding. A high evaluation of the significance of human personality has much the same effect. It also affects one's understanding of evil and suffering whether one sees the world as created perfect in the beginning, a Paradise from which we fell away by sin, or whether one sees it as eternally the same, a theatre or playground of struggle and illusion from which one seeks detachment or release, or whether one sees it as evolving or in process, gradually being fashioned into something perhaps perfectible in the future. Non-theistic religions have a different set of theoretical problems. Here it cannot be a matter of moral outrage at the nature of the world; for there is no one, ultimately speaking, to blame or rebuke. It is rather a matter of the correct discernment of the nature of things as they are and of whether it is possible to change them for the better or only to escape from them on to another plane.

Clearly, these differences in understanding and in the place and necessity of understanding will affect one's practical approaches to the problem of evil. It has been widely felt, for instance, that the pervasive Indian belief in rebirth and *karma*, which helps theoretical understanding by eliminating the supposition that suffering is undeserved, militates against practical action, especially to remedy social injustice, precisely because it renders that suffering intelligible. It is perfectly true that belief in *karma* encourages one to try to accumulate better *karma* for the future, and that this involves doing good to one's fellow men and women. But the question remains whether there can really be a dynamic impetus for social change within the framework of belief in *karma*. At all events, the Christian mind is more likely to hold that the recognition of un-deserved, innocent, suffering, crying out to God for redress, is a greater spur to practical action. But at this juncture our secular partners in dialogue will hasten to point out that it is religious beliefs, theistic or non-theistic, Western or Eastern, that blunt the edge of human practical response to evil. Marx's well-known statement that our task is not to understand the world but to change it has particular force here. For it looks as if the energies of religious people are likely to be diverted into trying to justify the ways of God with the world or to reach some transcendental plane where men and women can find release from the whole problem of evil and suffering. One can understand the protest of the secular mind that all we need is so to comprehend nature as to tame and master it as far as possible, and so to understand the human condition as to fight oppression, check the abuse of power and work co-operatively for the good of all.

But there is no such simple, short-cut, practical solution to the problem of evil. For the question of truth and falsity cannot be so easily bypassed. Secular ideologies themselves include understandings of the world and of human life which may be true or false. Our incentive and ability to change things are deeply affected by our fundamental beliefs about the existence or non-existence of God, the cyclical or historical nature of reality, the ultimacy or ephemeralness of personality, the availability or non-availability or spiritual resources from beyond the human world, and the actuality or non-actuality of an ultimate future goal or destiny for human life. So no apology is needed for exploring here the question of the practical overcoming of evil in the context of religious belief.

If practice is indeed embedded in belief, it behoves us, at this early stage in our reflections to explore more carefully the nature of the problem with which we are concerned. So far we have briefly indicated the twofold nature of the problem of evil – the problem of physical (and mental) suffering caused by natural evils, disasters, plagues, accidents and so on – and the problem of moral evil or human wickedness in all its forms, personal and collective. As far as natural evil is concerned, it is the appalling character of the suffering to which human beings (and animals) are susceptible, and also the sheer extent of such suffering, that constitute the problem. Of course, in every age, some attempts have been made to mitigate the effects of disease, accident and disaster. Much human energy and devotion have been spent on caring for the sick, on relief work, and on programmes to prevent epidemics and minimise vulnerability. Our own century has seen a vast increase, through the sciences of medicine, engineering and communications, in the scope of such work and in the possibilities of overcoming some at least of these evils. Yet the problem continues to baffle by its magnitude. Moreover, although we are aware of the existence of material resources and techniques of planning and social organisation that could remove want and foster security on a global scale, the difficulty of carrying this out, and of mobilising the political will to implement such policies, remains as great as ever.

We have suggested that religious beliefs determine or at least considerably affect people's reaction to these problems. Some quite basic religious beliefs encourage passivity and resignation in the face of natural evil. Admittedly it should be remembered that even these beliefs can bring some comfort and peace to individuals, but their overall effect is to increase the problem by inhibiting the will to change material and social conditions. Other religious beliefs have, on any reckoning, played a great part in inspiring men and women to dedicate their lives to the relief of suffering. Examples may be found in all three religions with which we are concerned both of beliefs encouraging resignation and of beliefs encouraging self-sacrificial devotion to humankind. It is not easy to judge whether the heart of Buddhism lies in techniques of meditation or in the fostering of compassion and practical relief work among the people. It is not easy to judge whether the heart of Christianity lies in other-worldly hope, or in such work as that of Mother Teresa in Calcutta. It is not easy to judge whether the heart of Hinduism lies in the practice of asceticism or devotion or in such social work as that of the Ramakrishna Mission. All one can say is that if we find ourselves assessing the religions by their capacity to produce and sustain movements and lives dedicated to the removal of the causes and effects of natural evil, we cannot avoid discrimination among the many beliefs embedded in these age-old religious traditions.

It is a curious fact that the problem of natural evil has evoked such different responses within each of our three religions. Buddhist conviction of the all-pervasiveness of suffering can have an inhibiting effect on social action; yet Buddhist denial of ego consciousness can inspire selfless compassion and dedication to others. Christian conviction that the world is destined for destruction can lead to concentration on personal salvation and future hope of heaven; yet Christian recognition of Christ's life and death as revelatory of God's love for humankind can produce lives of unreserved dedication to the welfare of the poor and the deliverance of the oppressed. Hindu conviction of the fundamentally illusory nature of the phenomenal world can encourage eventual withdrawal from every worldly task; yet Hindu belief that all men and women are one with Brahman can elicit selfless concern for those in need. Reflection on these curious anomalies in world religions may well lead our secular friends to repeat their claim that the natural evils of the human condition are best tackled by people free from all these conflicting religious beliefs and able, with uncluttered minds, to address themselves to the tasks in hand. But two questions must be put to such pragmatic secular minds: are they sure that people have the resources in themselves, without religion, for the selfless dedication required to devote themselves to the sick and the poor? And are they sure that they have the resources in themselves, without religion, to restrain and humanise their ideological and political commitment to the restructuring of human affairs? Reflection on these questions now leads us to consider the other main aspect of the problem of evil – that of moral evil or human wickedness, both individual and social.

Recent discussion in Western philosophy of religion has tended to focus on the Holocaust, the destruction by the Nazis of some six million Jews during the Second World War, as epitomising the problem of radical, extreme, moral evil. All the authors of the symposium, *Encountering*

Evil,[2] find themselves forced to contemplate this terrible event, as summing up, most powerfully, the moral objections raised in many people's minds to belief in an all-powerful benevolent God. That book, of course, typifies the Christian concentration on theodicy, on justifying the ways of God with humankind, and therefore on the theoretical rather than the practical aspect of the problem of evil. But we, with our particular interest in the practical aspect, cannot afford to neglect the extremities of human moral perversity as exemplified by the Holocaust. For no programme of action to make the world a better place, whether religiously motivated or not, can hope to commend itself, let alone succeed, unless it can be seen to take the measure of the worst that human beings can do and of human propensity to radical and monstrous evil. It is highly doubtful whether secular advocates of education and liberation have done justice to these depths of human moral evil. The insistence by Marxism that human nature could be changed by changing economic and social conditions has been proved naive by twentieth-century history. Bertrand Russell's hope[3] that education would remove the worst manifestations of the evil will – a view reflecting that of the ancient Greeks, for whom ignorance rather than moral evil was the basic problem – must likewise be called naive in the light of experience. But the religions, too, are far from agreed about the radical nature of moral evil. Buddhists, it seems, have more in common with the ancient Greeks in deeming ignorance to be the basic problem. Admittedly this ignorance is ignorance of the pervasive craving that characterises the endless round of rebirth. The Buddha's analysis of the human condition goes much further than anything attempted by the ancient Greeks. But it is far from clear that this craving, common to all sentient beings, and mirrored in natural energies below the level of sentience, is conceived by Buddhism in deeply moral terms. Human moral perversity or radical moral wickedness do not play a central role in this analysis. Nor is recognition of human propensity

---

[2] S. T. Davis (ed.), *Encountering Evil*, Edinburgh 1981.
[3] See, e.g. B. Russell, *Why I am Not a Christian*, London 1957, p. 42.

for radical evil a central insight in Hindu thought or devotion. Certainly the way of works is important in the Hindu *dharma*, and much can be made of this, as we shall see. But there is a tendency in Hinduism not only to restrict the scope of human action to the duties appropriate to one's place in society, but also to advocate the path of release through identification with the One or with the God beyond all distinctions, including those of good and evil. No doubt this tendency was interpreted in a somewhat unbalanced and extreme way by R. C. Zaehner in his last writings, the book, *Our Savage God,*[4] and the essay to be found in the posthumous collection, *The City Within the Heart.*[5] Zaehner seems to have become obsessed with the way in which religious penetration to levels allegedly beyond good and evil *could* result in remorseless wickedness of a particularly horrifying kind. At the same time he became deeply troubled by what he saw as the savage and amoral nature of the God of the Old Testament, despite that God's demand for moral good in his chosen people on earth. We mention Zaehner's rather unbalanced later views not in order to endorse them but to indicate the problems which the Christian mind tends to find in Eastern forms of spirituality and mysticism, the problem of a failure to grapple with what the Christian tradition calls man's sin, and a failure to treat the highest good in resolutely moral terms.

Not that Christianity is itself without ambiguity in this matter. Liberal Christians and Christian socialists, including Christian Marxists dedicated to the liberation of the oppressed, have all tended to underemphasise the radical nature of the problem of moral evil. An intriguing example may be drawn from the case of Teilhard de Chardin and from the startling change of mind about Teilhard which again R. C. Zaehner underwent in his last years. Zaehner delivered the Teape Lectures in India in 1969 on the topic, *Evolution in Religion.*[6] In those lectures he carried out a comparative study of Sri Aurobindo and Teilhard de Chardin, finding in their

[4] R. C. Zaehner, *Our Savage God*, London 1974.
[5] R. C. Zaehner, *The City Within the Heart*, London 1980.
[6] R. C. Zaehner, *Evolution in Religion*, Oxford 1971.

respective philosophies of evolution and progressive divinisation a point of convergence, and, despite some critical reservations, a common, basically optimistic, view of the eventual overcoming of evil through the forces of the spirit. But in his last writings, Zaehner repudiated Teilhard with remarkable vehemence not only for trying to bypass human evil but even for exonerating, in part at least, the spirit of fascism.[7] Many critics of Teilhard have agreed that he fails to reckon with the sheer wickedness of evil.

It is not surprising, then, that the most deeply reflective Christian minds have seen in human wickedness a greater problem than in natural evil, however horrific the latter's manifestations throughout the globe may be. It is true that the example of the Holocaust does not symbolise this problem with such terrible force even for Christians in the East as it does for Western Christians, in whose own history it has come to play so terrible a part. Indian Christians have expressed a sense of Western provincialism in such a reaction to the Holocaust. But other symbols, of just such devastating power, could doubtless be produced from within Indian history and culture to express the underlying truth that the human heart is 'deceitful above all things and desperately corrupt', as the prophet Jeremiah puts it (17.19). And no practical solution to the problem of evil that fails to point to genuine spiritual resources for overcoming radical moral evil will ever convince us for long of its greater effectiveness and power.

But now the question presents itself: is it realistic to suppose that evil *can* be overcome? In his book, *The Perfectibility of Man,*[8] John Passmore subjected all forms of utopianism to trenchant criticism for their unrealism and their tendency to bring great or even greater evils in their train, when attempts are made to make perfect people and societies essentially incapable of perfectibility. It will be remembered that the word 'utopia' literally means 'no place', and it is Passmore's view that all attempts, whether religious or secular, to implement utopian visions go against human nature and the world's nature and

---

[7] Zaehner, *Our Savage God,* pp. 26ff.
[8] J. Passmore, *The Perfectibility of Man,* London 1970.

only end in sacrificing countless human beings in the name of an unrealisable ideal. Better by far, on Passmore's view, to recognise that natural and moral evil are here to stay, and that all that can realistically be done is to minimise their effects by gradual, piecemeal, pragmatic policies and actions. This is a typical, Western, liberal view.

Once again we are faced here with a question of belief that may be true or may be false. And once again the secular debate, between the liberals for whom some gradual improvement in the human condition is the most that can be hoped for, and the Marxists, for whom human society is believed to be perfectible, is mirrored in many different ways both within and between the religions. Theravada Buddhism has certainly taught that it is possible for men and women to lead a moral life, and detailed instruction on such matters is a part of staple Buddhist doctrine as is instruction on the right ordering of human society. We shall see in the next chapter how such teaching has been developed, admittedly without much success, into forms of Buddhist socialism. Mahayana Buddhism has supplemented this ethical teaching with the religious idealism of the bodhisattva's compassion and the supernatural assistance of the celestial Buddhas. But the fundamental Buddhist teaching about the impermanence of all forms of reality and the ceaseless craving that produces universal suffering as the deepest and most pervasive truth about the phenomenal world militates against any utopian belief in the eventual overcoming of evil on earth. The higher ideals of Buddhism are of detachment and release from a condition that, in the most basic analysis, remains always the same. We shall notice, in the next chapter, some qualifications to this relatively pessimistic reading of Buddhism's approach to the question of perfectibility, but it seems clear that mainstream Buddhism has taken the view just described. Christianity, with its powerful eschatology, which it inherited from Judaism, has always included utopian strands and movements dedicated to transforming life on earth into the perfect society of the Kingdom of God. But the history of millenarianism does not inspire confidence in any Christian doctrine of the overcoming of evil here on earth. The main strands of Christianity, Catholic, Orthodox and Protestant, have all maintained a much more dialectical approach to the relationship between eschatological hope and individual and social ethics here on earth. The power of the Kingdom is at work, and we may hope and look for progress under divine providence towards the implementation of God's will on earth; but suffering and evil will only be finally overcome beyond death and beyond history in the new creation. Hinduism gives the appearance to Western commentators, at least, of being a much more static religion, sustaining a stable social order, and embracing all aspects of life on earth, evil as well as good, with the consolations of religion. In its more esoteric forms, Hinduism teaches a way of knowledge or of devotion that encourages the individual to transcend the world's suffering and evil in the dimension of the spirit. But again there is no suggestion that human social life on earth is perfectible or that the sufferings and evils to which human beings are vulnerable can ever as such be overcome. As pointed out already, the doctrine of *karma* tends to militate against this view.

All three religions, then, in their main historical forms appear to endorse a relatively pessimistic reading of the pervasiveness and permanence of suffering and evil. It seems to be characteristic of a religious response to human existence to suppose that only in the dimension of the spirit or in that of the eschatological future will evil finally be overcome. However, there are, clearly, different degrees of pessimism in the religions about what can be done to minimise human vulnerability and to improve the human condition, both individually and socially, and it is on these differences that we shall need to concentrate if we are to evaluate the contribution of the religions towards the overcoming of evil. The religions may be agreed that conditions on earth will never completely lack the sufferings caused by natural disasters and human wickedness, but they differ over what hope they extend and what resources they preach for the *partial* overcoming of evil on earth.

These reflections on whether it is realistic to suppose that evil can be overcome bring out the fact that our primary concern, in dwelling on practical responses to the world's evil, must be with what Dietrich Bonhoeffer calls the penultimate rather than the ultimate concerns of religion.[9] Indeed it is precisely because both millenarians and Marxists have blurred the distinction between realistic penultimate programmes and utopian ultimate hopes that they have caused such havoc in the course of history. For the most part the religions have avoided this confusion, and, in their penultimate concerns, taught much more sober and realistic approaches to the improvement of the conditions of life on earth. Unlike the liberal pragmatists, however, the religious schools of thought have set their individual and social ethical teachings in the context of their ultimate beliefs and hopes. And so the question remains how far people's ultimate beliefs promote or hinder their penultimate ethical concerns. This is really the chief problem with which these last three chapters are concerned. It is not a question of whether, within the world of the religions, there is to be found some blueprint for the complete overcoming of evil here on earth. It is rather a question of whether or not a religious perspective opens up dimensions of spiritual hope and makes available spiritual resources which can and do inspire, enhance and enable ethical advances in both individual and social life more creatively and more hopefully, though no less realistically, than do secular pragmatic views. As already stressed, questions of truth and falsehood are at stake here. Has a purely secular anthropology, in its liberal or its Marxist form, really understood human potentialities and limitations?

In the light of these considerations, let us look again at the issue of whether the main problem is natural evil and physical suffering or moral evil and human wickedness. Realism suggests that neither of these problems can be wholly overcome within human history on earth. Secular approaches and some religious approaches tend to concentrate on the quest for the elimination of suffering. It cannot be an objection that this is only a penultimate concern; for, as has just been argued,

---

[9] D. Bonhoeffer, *Ethics*, London 1955, Part 1, section IV.

it is the bearing of religions on our penultimate concerns with well being and justice that is at issue. The only objection to concentration on the practical problem of minimising people's natural vulnerabilities is the basically religious insight – though stressed in some religions more that in others – that moral and social evils are more deeply ingrained in human life than either reformers or revolutionaries tend to allow, and that, therefore, these moral evils (both individual and social) must be dealt with too, if any practical scheme for the betterment of the human condition is to have any hope of real success. On the other hand, religious preoccupation with the human heart – a preoccupation which has characterised much of historical Christianity – can lead to a reversal of priorities and a relatively low degree of importance being attached to the practical quest for a viable social ethic, designed to maximise human welfare.

A number of interrelated issues have emerged in the discussion so far and it is not easy to keep the right balance between them. We began by spelling out the depth and pervasiveness of the evils, both natural and moral, to which both individuals and societies are subject here on earth. We mentioned the ambiguity of the phenomenon of religion; but it is clear that we should try to concentrate on the best or most constructive ways in which the religions – and indeed the secular philosophies – have attempted to confront and cope with the world's ills. Despite our primary concern with the practical approaches to the problem of evil, we have stressed the question of the influence of theory or belief on practice, as well as on how people actually see the problem, and we have urged that there are questions or truth or falsity at stake here which must not be begged in advance. This was illustrated by a sketch of how the three religious traditions of Buddhism, Christianity and Hinduism have treated the question of where the main problem lies – with natural evil and suffering or with moral evil and wickedness. We then turned to the question of the realism or utopianism of belief that evil can be overcome, noting the relative realism of the religions, though a realism greatly affected by their ultimate beliefs.

With these reflections in mind, let us conclude this chapter by raising two further questions, on whose answers will depend how we are to proceed to investigate the practical contributions of the religions towards the overcoming of evil. The two questions are these: how far can study of religious traditions as they have been formed and transmitted in the past and as they manifest themselves today determine our assessment of their potentialities for future development *vis-à-vis* the overcoming of evil? And how far is it right to concentrate attention on the *differences* between the religions and on the *differences* between religious and secular approaches to the overcoming of evil?

The first of these two questions lead us to pursue the topic of religion and change. Religions are growing, developing, changing phenomena in world history. This is why Zaehner's Teape Lectures, to which we have already referred, were particularly interesting; for he selected for study and comparison two thinkers, Sri Aurobindo and Teilhard de Chardin, which, in their respective Hindu and Christian contexts, had developed dynamic, forward-looking, religious philosophies, not least in the light of the modern theory of evolution. Yet even Zaehner has been criticised for the way in which he was wont to assess the significance and power of religious traditions other than his own. Zaehner had an encyclopaedic knowledge of the sacred texts and traditions of the religions. Probably he knew far more than most Buddhists and Hindus of the details of their scriptures and schools down the ages. But just because of this encyclopaedic knowledge, he was, notwithstanding his interest in Aurobindo, less sensitive to modern developments, reinterpretations and potentialities within the great world faiths and more inclined to assess them by the content of their scriptures and traditions. But when we think of Hinduism, for example, we are reckoning with a vast array of beliefs, schools and practices that have it in them to produce not only an Aurobindo, but a Tagore, a Vivekananda, a Gandhi and a Radhakrishnan. Of course, we cannot help asking how faithful these creative figures were to the traditions out of which they sprang, and perhaps more pertinently, how typical they were. But it is hardly the place of Western scholars to refuse to accept such figures as authentically Hindu. One is reminded of Walter Kaufmann's reluctance to accept Reinhold Niebuhr's work as exemplifying an authentically Christian ethics, since it differed so much from the Bible.[10] It is much easier for outsiders to disagree with something relatively fixed and static. But it is one of the lessons of the phenomenology of religion for the philosophy of religion that we have to let the inner developments of the religions and their power to adapt and change in new circumstances come within the horizon of our awareness as we make comparisons and appraisals, in our case, of their resources for the overcoming of evil. Of course, there must be some continuity between the old and the new in any tradition of faith. It cannot be that anything at all can count as Buddhist ethics or Christian ethics or Hindu ethics. Thus we shall find in each tradition attempts being made to relate the innovations and creative advances, not least in social concern, to the scriptures and traditions, as, supposedly, eliciting and expressing the heart or inner meaning of those scriptures and traditions. In the final two chapters, we shall be particularly concerned to inquire how traditional Buddhist, Christian and Hindu concepts and ideas have been reinterpreted and applied to the quest for social justice in our time. In each of these religions such developments have involved a great deal of effort in wrestling with and reinterpreting the traditions; and of course, they are very controversial. Many Christians, for example, think Latin American liberation theology a betrayal of the gospel. But others see in such movements an authentic insight into or recovery of the gospel of the love of God for every human being and especially for the poor and the oppressed. Comparative religious ethics seeks to trace and compare similar developments within all the great religions.

This question of religion and change and of how we are to evaluate both the potential and the authenticity of modern Buddhist, Christian and Hindu attempts to do something about the world's suffering and evil is not just a matter of each religion's separate internal developments and changes. A

---

[10] See W. Kaufmann, *Critique of Religion and Philosophy*, New York 1958, section 68.

major feature of the contemporary history of religions is the interaction of the different faiths with each other and with the secular revolutions, scientific, technological and political, of our age. It can hardly be denied that it is these interactions and the mutual pressures which they have entailed that have stimulated the religions to develop new forms of social ethics and new ways of applying their traditions of spirituality to all the concerns of human life. But it would be unfair to say that the traffic is all one way and that the religions are simply reacting, rather desperately, to the impact of modernity. Quite apart from the theory, mentioned earlier that the scientific and political revolutions of the Renaissance, Enlightenment and post-Enlightenment worlds are themselves products of a particular religious tradition, it is clear that we are dealing here with a two-way flow of traffic between religion and modernity. As we shall see, this is not just a matter of subjecting the harsher aspects of the scientific, technological and political revolutions of our time to penetrating criticism in the light of the dimension of the spirit. It is also a matter of discovering in the religions themselves powerful ethical and spiritual resources for the overcoming of evil.

The other question raised for preliminary consideration at this stage was; How far is it right to concentrate on *differences* between religions and on *differences* between religious and secular approaches to the overcoming of evil? Once again it might seem that the sheer weight of suffering and evil in the world, demanding remedy and redress, ought to lead all men and women of good will, of all religions or of none, to co-operate together in practical social and political action to meet human needs and make the world a better place. Undoubtedly this is true, and indeed, for the Christian, there are good theological reasons, as M. M. Thomas, among others, has pointed out, for recognising the meeting-point of the religions and the quasi-religions or secular ideologies in humanity and its basic needs.[11] Christians will indeed look for God at work and for Christ's presence in all attempts to humanise the world, whether self-consciously religious or

[11] M. M. Thomas, *Man and the Universe of Faiths*, Madras 1975.

not. But sadly, recognition of this joint commitment to social justice and human welfare is not enough. It occurs, where it does occur, at much too general a level. It may provide an acceptable framework within which to pursue the question of how suffering and evil are to be overcome, but it goes nowhere near deep enough into the detailed practicalities of how the world and the human condition are to be changed, and, even more seriously, of how men and women are to be sustained in their commitment to changing the world. Such overall general agreement to work together for the good of all is not nearly enough to enable us to overcome the problems confronting the human race. And even such a general agreed framework is not easy to reach, at least if it is to mean more than paying lip service to a vague ideal. We still have to face the question of human selfishness and greed, and of the resources available to human beings to enable them to dedicate themselves to the common good. And within that framework, we still have to locate the deepest needs of human beings on earth, and weigh the claims of individuals against society or the State, of individual freedom against the collectivity. The religious mind is bound to question the adequacy of the secular mind on all these issues.

Between the religions, too, agreement to co-operate for the common good is easy to achieve at the level of vague generality. But again the religions themselves differ in how they discern need, in their respective valuation of personal and social life, and in their understanding of the resources available to men and women for the overcoming of evil. S. C. Thakur, in his useful book, *Christian and Hindu Ethics*,[12] tries to play down these differences where Christianity and Hinduism are concerned. Despite their different understandings of the nature and the destiny of humankind, he claims, the virtues and the moral policies and attitudes encouraged by the two religions are strikingly similar. But we need to press more deeply than this, and ask just how similar are Buddhist compassion, Christian love and Hindu non-violence. Do these virtues really manifest themselves in qualitatively similar

---

[12] S. C. Thakur, *Christian and Hindu Ethics*, London 1969.

action? Moreover we need to ask whether the fostering of attitudes and virtues is really the heart of the matter where the overcoming of evil is concerned. In the next chapter, we shall explore this latter problem in some detail. For one of the main problems for religious ethics in the contemporary world – and this is true of Buddhist, Christian and Hindu ethics – is whether training in the virtues should be their main contribution to making the world a better place or whether there is not an equal need for a specifically religious commitment to the re-ordering of social, political and economic life.

11

Individual or society?

In concentrating attention on what is to be done about the world's ills and what practical resources are to be found in the religions towards the overcoming of evil, we must face up to the question whether the heart of the problem, as the religions see it, lies with the individual or with society. This question is not at all easy to answer, especially if we take into account the great changes and developments in all religious traditions that have come about through their interaction with each other and with the scientific, technological and political revolutions of the modern world. In the pre-modern centuries, there would have been little doubt that in each of our three religions the heart of the problem was thought to lie with the individual. Buddhism, Christianity and Hinduism all preached ways of salvation or liberation for the individual. In Buddhism, the Noble Eightfold Path is a path towards enlightenment for each human being as he or she becomes aware of the prevalence of suffering, its cause, and how he or she may pass beyond its endless chain. In Christianity it is the individual's acceptance of forgiveness and atonement through the cross of Christ that sets him or her, by God's grace, on the path to salvation and communion with the Lord. In Hinduism, whether through the way of works, the way of devotion or the way of knowledge, it is the individual who finally achieves release into oneness or identity with the all-pervading Spirit. Much may also be said in each of these religions about the right ordering of society and in fact for much of their histories Buddhism, Christianity and Hinduism have all been relatively conservative, stabilising, factors where human society has been concerned, but few (except certain sociologists such as Emile Durkheim) would have claimed that this function represented the essential heart of any of these three religions.

Now, by contrast, we find in the modern age profound and serious attempts being made to re-interpret the essential core of each of these religions as bearing directly on the question of social justice. And social ethics is being seen, not as a relatively subsidiary consequence of a religious perception of reality, but as belonging to the very heart of each religion's concept of salvation or liberation.

It may well be suggested that this development has gone furthest in Christianity. Indeed many people think it has gone too far. Latin American liberation theology, whether Catholic or Protestant, has been accused of forsaking the Christian gospel by actually identifying the salvation which Christ brings with the liberation of the poor and the oppressed from the structures of injustice in which they find themselves entrapped. But even where this trend of radical reinterpretation of the heart of the Christian message as equating liberation with social revolution is criticised, as it was by Pope John Paul II in his speech to the Latin American bishops' conference at Pueblo in 1979, we still find a strong emphasis on Christian commitment to social justice being taught, if not as the essence of Christianity, then at least as its *necessary* consequence. Similarly the World Council of Churches, although in its more recent General Assemblies it has somewhat qualified the radical pronouncements made at Uppsala (1968) and Bangkok (1973), still endorses a radical social ethic of support and work for liberation movements throughout the world.[1] Christianity, then, at the present stage of its history and development, includes powerful strands of commitment to radical social policies of large-scale structural change, as part of its practical response to human suffering and evil.

Similar developments can be traced in modern Buddhism and modern Hinduism as well. In Buddhist lands such as

[1] The bearing of these trends on the Indian situation and the demands that they make on the Indian Christian Churches have been discussed by M. M. Thomas in *Religion and the Revolt of the Oppressed*, Delhi 1981.

Burma and Sri Lanka, not only has much effort been expended on training schemes both for Buddhist monks and lay folk in social service, but there have also been some attempts to work out, on Buddhist principles, political programmes explicitly referred to as Buddhist socialism. Their relative lack of success in the 1980s and 90s should not be allowed to obscure the principle behind such developments. The Hindu Renaissance too has produced remarkable movements dedicated both to social service and to social and political reform, from Vivekananda and the Ramakrishna Mission, through Gandhi and the Sarvodaya movement, into the present.

The question arises, of course, how far these developments in social ethics and social and political concern may be understood not only as authentic fruits of their respective religious traditions, but as genuinely religious phenomena. We may ask, of Buddhist socialism, for example, not only was it really Buddhist, but was it really a religious response. We may ask of Christian liberation theology not only has it been authentically Christian but also has it been more than a secular ideology in Christian garb. We may ask of Gandhi's eventual opposition to caste divisions not only whether it was an authentically Hindu development, but also whether it simply reflected encounter with secular egalitarian ideals.

It is easier to rebut the charge that these developments represent alien secular incursions into traditional religions than it is to rebut the charge that the historical religions are tending to lose their distinctive identity. This is perhaps easiest to show in the case of Gandhi and Vinoba Bahve; for if ever there were religiously motivated movements for social and political reform they were Gandhi's and Vinoba's. The principles of soul-force and truth-force are quintessentially religious principles, and the social thought of the Sarvodaya movement was deliberately advanced as an alternative to the purely political movements of our time. Buddhist socialism, too, although it may have required the stimulus of secular socialism to activate it, for the most part represented itself as a distinctive alternative to Marxist policies and relied on a specifically religious analysis of humankind's basic nature and predicament. Christian liberation theology, like Christian socialism before it, far from being no more than a pale reflection of modern secular political movements, as Edward Norman would have it be,[2] is deeply rooted in the revealed will of God and in a thoroughly religious conception of our future destiny in the Kingdom of God. Indeed, the case of Christianity is doubly complex, if it is true, as is sometimes argued, that egalitarian secular ideologies have themselves as a fact of history sprung from the Judaeo-Christian tradition. Christian ethics may now involve a religious critique of secular ideologies, but at the same time it recognises itself in secularised form in those ideologies as well as being their historical source.

More will be said about the religious nature of Buddhist, Christian and Hindu social ethics in the final chapter, when we come to look more closely at religious resources for the overcoming of evil. But having rejected the suggestion that these modern developments are purely secular in inspiration, we turn now to the more telling objection that these contemporary social – often socialist – versions of Buddhism, Christianity and Hinduism have lost touch with their respective traditions and transformed them into something unrecognisable. It is at this point that the question of the historical interaction of the religions becomes important. For it has been argued that it is Christianity's impact on the other world faiths that has led them to discover within themselves the possibility of more radical forms of social ethics. In other words, while there is a problem over the genuinely Christian nature of Christian political theology, there is a further problem of the influence of Christianity on Buddhist and Hindu political ethics.

These problems cannot be resolved empirically; for one is not trying simply to assess diverse religious phenomena which can be pointed to as manifesting the essence of empirical Buddhism, Christianity or Hinduism. One is talking rather of potentialities for growth and change under mutual interaction and influence and in response to the challenges of modernity.

[2] See E. R. Norman, *Christianity and the World Order*, Oxford 1979.

The point can be brought out if we compare this question of comparative social ethics with John Hick's global theology of religion. As is well known, Hick has been advancing, over recent decades, a theory of religious pluralism which gives more or less equal significance to the major world religions as ways of salvation or spiritual blessedness for men and women who find themselves born and brought up within their respective orbits.[3] The same many-sided, ultimate reality, according to Hick, is experienced salvifically in each of the mainstreams of world religion. Part of Hick's evidence for this pluralistic global theology is the empirical fact of comparable forms of spirituality and devotion in the different religions. He points to hymns and devotional literature from all the main religious traditions as manifestly expressive of the same kind of religious experience, and to the phenomenon of sanctity fostered in them all, as indicative of life-transforming power. This method of assessing the significance of the world religions can, of course, be questioned. It is not our intention to debate it here.[4] The present point is simply that this empirical method of substantiating the case for religious pluralism is not nearly so easy to apply to the question of comparative religious social ethics. For we are considering relatively recent developments, subsequent to the main phases of the historical encounter of religions, and indeed we are considering relative potentialities for future development. When the question was put – in the course of a Cambridge seminar – whether the different religions have it in them, out of their own resources, to develop viable and persuasive forms of religious social ethics, Hick replied that the different religions were at different stages of historical development and that Buddhism, Hinduism and Islam could not be assessed for their social ethical potential by the evidence of their past and present attitudes, any more than medieval Christianity could have been assessed for its potential then. If this is so, then comparative social ethics is a very different matter from comparative spirituality. In the case of

---

[3] See J. H. Hick, *An Interpretation of Religion*, London 1989.
[4] See ch. 9 above.

spirituality we examine scriptures, hymns, writing and the lives of spiritual masters. The data are, in a fairly wide sense, empirically available. In the case of social ethics, we are examining potentialities and resources for development and change. This is much harder to do, and is clearly a much less empirical procedure.

In order to substantiate this point let us examine both the reasons why some doubts have been expressed about the potential of these religions to foster a dynamic social ethic and also the ways in which their characteristic doctrines have nevertheless been developed and interpreted in social ethical terms.

It is not difficult to understand why Buddhism has been thought by many to lack a positive, dynamic, social ethic. From the early Buddhist texts and from the history of Theravada Buddhism at least, we get the impression both of deep pessimism about life in this world, including social relations, and also of a powerful concentration of the individual's path to liberation. The pervasive *karma/samsara* doctrines and the diagnosis of the human predicament as that of suffering brought about by craving seem to militate against the idea of radical social transformation. Even a modern Buddhist, such as H. Saddhatissa, writes very negatively of politics (by contrast with religion) as inevitably a matter of the acquisition and exertion of power by one group over another.[5] Conversely, the ultimate religious ideal, release into Nirvana, seems incommensurate with social life, however well ordered, let alone with placing a high value on social transformation. Even such a well-disposed student of religion as Paul Tillich, who took part in dialogue with Mahayana Buddhists in Japan, wrote, 'No belief in the new in history, no impulse for transforming society can be derived from the principle of Nirvana'.[6] And similarly John Robinson, in his Teape Lectures, published as *Truth is Two-Eyed*,[7] sees a tendency towards inner concentration rather than social awakening in the Buddhist traditions.

[5] H. Saddhatissa, *Buddhist Ethics: Essence of Buddhism*, New York 1970.
[6] P. Tillich, *Christianity and the Encounter of World Religions*, New York 1963, p. 73.
[7] J. A. T. Robinson, *Truth is Two-Eyed*, London 1979.

However, in trying to do justice to the actual social teachings of Buddhism and to the possible developments in interpretation of its key religious ideas, we have to note a number of factors which might lead us to qualify this initial pessimistic reading of Buddhism as a source of social transformation. We are not only referring here to the place of right action in the Noble Eightfold Path and its application down the ages in Buddhist teaching about the family and the State, nor to the modern Buddhist emphasis on social service and the care of the poor and the sick. We are referring also to the special qualities of life which Buddhism has fostered down the centuries, the compassion, gentleness and serenity, which are rightly associated with Buddhist practice. But, since, as stressed in the previous chapter, such practices and qualities of life are embedded in beliefs and doctrines, we will be especially interested in the way in which it is *argued* that, despite initial appearances, the key Buddhist *doctrines* in fact have important social ethical implications. For example, it is argued that the 'no-self doctrine' of classical Buddhism provides the theoretical basis not only for selfless action but also for strict egalitarianism. Moreover the concept of *jivanmukti* or living liberation, as Ninian Smart has argued,[8] can be used to counter the suggestion that the Buddhist way constitutes a kind of flight from reality. On the contrary, the attainment of detachment and liberation from craving enables the Buddhist to live and work, compassionately, for universal brotherhood. Indeed the concept of Nirvana itself has been held to imply 'a life of unceasing brotherliness in the pure atmosphere of truth, goodness, freedom and enlightenment'. Those are the words of Lakshmi Narasu, quoted by M. M. Thomas in *Man and the Universe of Faiths*.[9] In the same chapter, Thomas refers to a converse point, namely the Buddhist objection to theism as 'the deepest root of dictatorship' (an objection, incidentally, echoed by Don Cupitt in *Taking Leave of God*.)[10]

[8] N. Smart, 'Living Liberation: Jivanmukti and Nirvana', in E. J. Sharpe and J. R. Hinnells (eds.), *Man and His Salvation. Studies in Memory of S. G. F. Brandon*, Manchester 1973.

[9] M. M. Thomas, *Man and the Universe of Faiths*, Madras 1975, p. 90.

[10] D. Cupitt, *Taking Leave of God*, London 1980.

These considerations might lead us to suppose that Buddhism is well placed to foster humane social relations and to counter the abuse of power.

The issue before us at present is not so much the question whether there is a desirable complementarity between Christianity and Buddhism – Christianity preaching social dynamism and active love, Buddhism preaching non-violence and detached compassion (a thesis advocated by Ninian Smart in his Gifford Lectures, *Beyond Ideology*)[11] – but rather whether Buddhism can itself become the source of social transformation and the overcoming of evil at the level of social and political action as well as at that of individual selflessness. We have seen reasons for supposing that Buddhism has this potential, that the 'lotus of the doctrine' can be unfolded in this way.

However, some doubts remain. It is not just that Buddhism, like other faiths, still teaches that the betterment of society comes about only through the betterment of individuals. This is a common religious theme and we will be considering it at the end of this chapter. It is rather a matter of two more fundamental doubts about Buddhism's capacity to sustain a dynamic ethic of social change. In the first place, the no-self doctrine, for all its egalitarian potential, seems to have a very negative effect where our appreciation of the significance and worth of human persons, human activity and human aspirations are concerned. It has been remarked that Buddhist values hardly justify the modern emphasis on human *rights*. Nor is it easy to see how the quest for enlightenment, whether for oneself or for others or even for all, can enable men and women to find in interpersonal relations and in social practices themselves something of irreducible and permanent value. In the second place, the lack in mainstream Buddhist thought of an ultimate vision of the future, couched in social terms, is also a factor that might be thought to inhibit the development of a strong social ethic. So while it is possible for Buddhists to speak of universal brotherhood and indeed to make much more of the eschatological figure of the 'Buddha-

[11] N. Smart, *Beyond Ideology*, London 1981.

to-be', the question remains whether the basic concepts and values of Buddhism really support or demand a radical ethic of social change.

Christianity too has often been interpreted as an inward-looking, other-worldly, religion. The New Testament, much more than the Old, concentrates on the inner transformation effected by the divine Spirit (through faith in Christ crucified and risen); and while the fruits of the Spirit, including love, peace, kindness, gentleness, are much stressed in New Testament teaching, the main focus of Christian hope lies in the future 'coming' of Christ in glory at the end of the present age, and the perfected kingdom of the resurrection world. The early Christians, like the early Buddhists, were pretty pessimistic about the historical future. At first the most that could be hoped for from the political structures of the day was an ordered framework within which Christian mission and Christian community could grow. In this sense it was argued that 'the powers that be are ordained of God' (Rom 13.1). Later, within the conversion of Constantine, the vision and hope of a Christianised world came to replace this relatively pessimistic view, but again it was a hope for social change through the conversion and betterment of individuals (especially of powerful and influential individuals, such as kings and emperors). But throughout the medieval and the Reformation periods, the mainstream Christian churches continued to teach an otherworldly eschatology – a radical transformation only in the beyond. By contrast with minority millenarian groups, the Catholic, Protestant and Orthodox churches, while admittedly teaching a social ethic for all, based on divine law or divine ordinances, concentrated their energies on individual faith and spirituality, on specifically Christian communities, whether monastic or congregational, and on personal charity and good works.

However, the factors making for more radical forms of social ethics and indeed for the reinterpretation of basic doctrines in social ethical terms are much easier to trace in the case of Christianity than in that of Buddhism. The Old Testament exodus motif and prophecies about God's love of justice, the Magnificat and Christ's preaching to the poor and outcast in the New Testament, the Christian doctrine of the Incarnation and God's solidarity, in the Person of his Son, with suffering humanity, and above all the command to love one's neighbour as oneself, contain the seeds of a Christian imperative to work for social justice that, not surprisingly, have led in the modern period to forms of Christian socialism and the theology of liberation. Moreover Christian eschatology, with its dominant symbols of the Kingdom of God and the Communion of Saints, has proved capable of making a powerful critical impact on present social systems, and inspiring dedicated work for social justice and a new social and economic order. Millenarian attempts to implement these ideas directly may have proved utopian, even disastrous, but the power of Christian eschatological symbols has been and continues to be very great.

Even in Christianity's case, however, some doubts remain. For all his stress on the Christian formation of social conscience, the Pope's insistence, in his speech at Pueblo, that we must distinguish authentically Christian liberation from liberation based on 'ideologies that rob it of consistency with an evangelical view of man' is hard to gainsay. What the Pope calls 'an evangelical view of man' was spelled out earlier in the speech in terms of the Church's teaching that each individual in made in God's image, yet in need of personal redemption. So to translate soteriology into collectivist ideology is to lose touch with the essence of Christianity.

When we turn to the many-faceted phenomenon of Hinduism, we encounter similar problems of assessing its traditional core and its potentiality for development to those we found in the case of Buddhism. It is not difficult to understand why Hinduism has been thought by many to lack a positive, creative social ethic. In its more philosophical forms, it has appeared to urge the ultimate ideal for the individual of release from the round of rebirth through the way of knowledge. In its more popular forms, its social structure and devotional cults have appeared to lack the moral and social dynamism of ethical monotheism and prophetic religion. Even the Bhagavadgita, with its devotional fervour and its emphasis on the way of action, has appeared to commend complete detachment in the performance of caste duty and a union of the devotee with the Lord that passes beyond the sphere of good and evil. Moreover some modern Indian writers on Hinduism have urged the complete secularisation of social and political concern and their total separation from religion. Thus N. K. Devaraja, in his book *Hinduism and the Modern Age*, states categorically that 'religion is a matter of the personal spiritual needs of man', and that 'its interference with socio-political and legal institutions should be reduced to a minimum'.[12]

On the other hand, the Hindu renaissance, in the persons of such men as Ram Mohun Roy, Ramakrishna and Vivekananda, not only exemplified the emergence and development of a much more urgent social and political concern within Hinduism itself, but also the way in which characteristic Hindu teachings about the soul and its relation to the ultimate reality behind or at the heart of things can themselves be reinterpreted to justify and demand equality and justice. Thus Vivekananda based his commitment to social reform on the doctrine of the oneness of all souls with the Spirit that pervades the universe, and he dealt with the problem of caste by giving it a functional meaning, and teaching that the ideal is for everyone to become Brahmin. Similarly Gandhi eventually came to reject caste altogether on the basis of an understanding of the divine truth and love that constitute the fundamental law of all life. Indeed Gandhi's positive interpretation of the ancient Indian concept of *ahimsa* (non-violence) may be regarded as indicative of Hinduism's most powerful spiritual resource for the overcoming of evil.

The question of the social-political potentialities of Hinduism is illuminated by consideration of Sarvepalli Radhakrishnan's reply to the well-known criticism of Hinduism by Albert Schweitzer. In a number of his books, Schweitzer had argued that Hinduism never quite succeeded in achieving a vital and irresolvable ethical stance.[13] The Upanishadic search for release from the world through esoteric knowledge,

[12] N. K. Devaraja, *Hinduism and the Modern Age*, Bombay 1975, p. 132.
[13] See, e.g. A. Schweitzer, *Christianity and the Religions of the World*, London 1923.

popular Hindu cultic piety, and even the Bhagavadgita's teaching on the spirit of detachment with which one should carry out one's duty just because all is in God, militate against conviction of an absolute and categorical ethical demand to love the neighbour for his own sake. Radhakrishnan replies to this criticism in his book, *Eastern Religion and Western Thought*,[14] by denying that the path of mysticism and spiritual transcendence constitutes a threat to ethics. On the contrary, ethics is the indispensable pre-requisite for the attainment of spiritual perfection, and indeed, by doing away with selfishness and fostering *ahimsa*, spiritual transcendence promotes the welfare of the world. 'The mystic', says Radhakrishnan, 'has a burning passion for social righteousness.'[15]

It is not easy to evaluate this reply. Radhakrishnan still sees human spiritual destiny as more than ethical goodness, though he insists that it cannot be achieved without it. We may well wonder whether this relative assessment of the significance of the ethical is sufficient to sustain 'a burning passion for social righteousness'. A passion for social righteousness surely requires unconditional commitment to human rights, to persons as uniquely valuable, and to social relations as of the essence of humanity. All these values still seem threatened by the higher place of spiritual trans-cendence in Radhakrishnan's scheme of things; for that spiritual transcendence is apparently not itself conceived of in social terms.

At all events, it seems clear that modern Hinduism, like modern Buddhism, looks to the transformation of society only in and through the transformation of the individual. To that extent, Hinduism too locates the heart of the problem of evil in the individual rather than society itself.

This has widely been held to be the characteristically religious response to the practical problem of evil. For as we saw, Christianity too addresses the heart and soul of the individual as the place where transformation must first occur.

[14] S. Radhakrishnan, *Eastern Religion and Western Thought*, London 1939.
[15] Radhakrishnan, *Eastern Religion and Western Thought*, p. 109.

When we compare the three religions with which we are concerned with the more collectivist approach of Marxism, we may well be struck by their common perception of the need to deal first with the evil that is in us if ever social evils are to be overcome. And all three religions share a deep distrust of the collectivists' apparent willingness to sacrifice the individual and to ride roughshod over many individuals in the interests of radical social change and the eventual communist state. To continue this list of what the religions unite in finding wanting in collectivist secular ideologies, there is also their failure to recognise, let alone to cope with, the problem of power and the abuse of power, and, of course, their failure to have anything to say about the all-pervasive fact of death. The religions, by contrast – to take these points in reverse order – speak of the overcoming or transcendence of death; they speak of spiritual and ethical restraints upon the exercise of power; they appeal to the individual soul, thereby refusing to endorse its subordination to the State or to the future; and, above all, they seek to enable men and women to eradicate the evil or the ignorance or the craving that corrupts human life from within. When we contrast religious approaches to the overcoming of evil, therefore, with secular collectivist approaches, we may be more aware of their common approach than of their mutual differences.

But enough has been said already to make us question any easy or superficial assimilation here. We may have found in the religions a common recognition that the heart of the problem lies as much within the individual as with the social system, so that to bypass the individual in concentrating on social change leaves the deepest problem unresolved. Yet when we turn back to the religions themselves and to their respective diagnoses of that problem and their suggested cures, comparative study discloses considerable differences in understanding and evaluation which are bound to affect their ability to foster social ethical concern. Even their concern with the individual differs (as has already been pointed out) according to the seriousness with which they face up to the radical moral evil in the human heart; but their concern with society differs, too, and is bound to differ, according to the relatively high or low evaluation they place on human interpersonal and social life as such. In order to demonstrate this point we may single out, for further comment, four aspects of human social life, on which the religions clearly differ in their assessments of human nature and destiny. These are: 1: the importance of the body; 2: the significance of the person; 3: the ultimacy of interpersonal and social life; and 4: the final goal of human existence.

1. The importance of the human body for any social ethical concern is very great. Our basic physical needs are obviously the first object of attention in social ethics. People need food, shelter and clothing; the lack of these things constitutes a major evil to be overcome. The human body can also be the victim of terrible accidents and diseases, and of appalling cruelty in war and torture. The prevention or cure of these evils is another major objective of social ethics. Now religious attitudes to these evils have been very various and have changed greatly over time. On the one hand, the religions have taught selfless love, compassion, non-violence, the care and cure of the sick, the feeding of the hungry. On the other hand, some religious doctrines have led to a despising or neglect of the body, or worse still a willingness to maim or to burn in the interests of some higher religious goal. Of course, it is a function of religion to draw attention to other human needs than the physical and it may well be that exclusive concentration on physical need brings great spiritual deprivation in its train, as we have seen in both modern Western consumer society and in communist forced collectivisation. Moreover it is quite proper to speak of higher needs and values than the physical. But a religion's potential for fostering social ethics will undoubtedly in part depend on or be conditioned by its evaluation of the body – as a tomb, an illusion, or a temple of the spirit or whatever – and on whether its doctrines of emanation or creation or incarnation encourage us to value the body and cherish it. Treatment of this theme will be continued in the next chapter when we consider the religions' attitudes to

sexuality – a sphere where great evils have been perpetrated over the centuries, sometimes in the name of religion.

2. The significance of the body is only one aspect of the significance of the person, and here too the religions differ greatly, despite their apparent agreement on fostering the virtues of love and compassion. It is an extraordinary fact that apparently similar egalitarian and compassionate teaching can be drawn from such diverse doctrines as the Buddhist no-self doctrine, the 'that art thou' doctrine of the Vedanta, and the Christian doctrine of man and woman made in the image of God. The fact of such widely different justifications of social solidarity may suggest again to some that the religious doctrines are redundant; all that matters are equality and love. But once again we should look more closely at what precisely is meant in the different religious traditions by terms such as equality, love, compassion or non-violence. Does not disagreement over the ultimate value of personal being affect our understanding of equality and human rights, and of what it means to love our fellow human beings? These questions will be considered further in the final chapter. But we will find ourselves expressing some doubts about the Buddhist ideal of compassion just because the value of human personality seems to be undermined by the no-self doctrine. Indeed compassion for all suffering beings, human and non-human (taken to even further extremes in Jainism, of course) seems further to reduce the positive significance of persons as such. Conversely Gandhi's inspired characterisation of the outcasts as Harijans – children of God – exemplifies the way in which in this case the socially disadvantaged can be seen as of worth and of value within a particular religious frame of reference (although this characterisation has not in fact had as much effect as Gandhi hoped and is now resented by the Harijans themselves). But to see human beings as children of God and as loved by God is a way of bringing out the value of persons; and to focus these ideas especially on the poor is a powerful source and reinforcement of social ethical concern. That Gandhi's humanism is no isolated phenomenon in Indian culture is indicated by the fact that both Buddhism (in the Mahayana

school) and Hinduism (in the Gita and later commentaries) have developed forms of humanistic personalism.[16]

The significance of persons is, of course, central to Christianity where men and women are held to be made in the image of God, loved by God, and called to be children of God. Now in the comparative study of religions we need to probe such similarities further. It appears that in both Christianity and Hinduism the significance and worth of persons are enhanced by their status as children of God. But as well as asking how central and pervasive these ideas are, or are becoming, in their respective religious contexts, we need to explore the nature of this love of God that gives each person – and especially the poor – such high significance. A comparison of the gospels and the Bhagavadgita, for example, may yield striking similarities, but it may yield striking differences too in the way in which God's love for us is conceived. We need to ask how these differences over the concept of God's love affect the way in which people as children of God are understood and treated.

3. We turn now to the third aspect of our problem, namely the religions' different conceptions of the importance of human social relations themselves. We have argued that different attitudes to the body and different attitudes to the person are bound to affect the way in which, within a given religious tradition, the sphere of social ethics is approached. This obviously applies even more strongly to different attitudes to personal and social relationships as such. We are not just referring here to traditional Buddhist, Christian and Hindu teaching on the family and the State, which, as already acknowledged, has never been absent from any of these religions and has undoubtedly contributed to the relative stability of human life in many areas of the world over many centuries. We are referring rather to the question of the centrality of interpersonal relation in the religions' different conceptions of what it is to be human. For surely the cruciality

---

[16] Its somewhat unstable presence in Indian religion is discussed by Richard de Smet in his essay, 'Towards an Indian View of the Person', in M. Chatterjee (ed.), *Contemporary Indian Philosophy*, Series Two, London 1974.

of a religion's commitment to social justice depends on whether it sees community as belonging to the essence of humanity at its highest and that means its most spiritual levels. All too often in the past, religion has been thought of, on Plotinian terms, as the flight of the alone to the alone or in Whiteheadian terms as what the individual does with his solitariness. If enlightenment is thought of as the goal of an inward solitary path, if salvation is thought of as the solitary soul's 'at-one-ment' with his Maker, if release from the round of rebirth means passing beyond all human fellowship as well as beyond all earthly suffering, then it seems that the inner dynamic of religion is being concentrated on a path ultimately inimical to social ethical concern. It may be replied that only the few in fact tread the path of solitariness, leave their families and friends behind, and venture on the life of the ascetic, the hermit or the wanderer in the forest. But if such paths are thought of as the highest ideal in religion, and spirituality conceived in terms of such ideals, then it is hard to see how social ethics can be anything but a relatively subsidiary concern.

In his Gifford Lectures, *Religion and the One*,[17] F. C. Copleston argues that theism is better adapted than monism to a socially oriented ethic, for it envisages as the goal of creation a unified human society, to be created by us in co-operation with God. And this central ideal of theistic religion acts as a spur towards the realisation of that ideal. It is not bypassed nor transcended in the interests of some allegedly higher ideal. But Copleston is clearly thinking only of a certain sort of theism. There have been varieties of theism, Christian as well as Hindu, that have exalted the solitary path to knowledge of God above that of the social dimension. So Copleston's point can only be sustained in respect of certain sorts of theism, namely those that conceive of men and women as in essence relational beings, made in the image of a God who is himself conceived in relational terms. An example would be Karl Barth's Christian anthropology, with its understanding of man as essentially

---

[17] F. C. Copleston, *Religion and the One*, London 1982.

'man for others', and as such reflecting his Creator, the Triune God.[18]

4. This theological reinforcement of social conceptions of the human occurs not only where doctrines of creation are concerned, but also, as Copleston points out, with respect to eschatology. This brings us to the fourth aspect of the religions' understanding of the situation being singled out for further consideration, namely their different conceptions of the final goal of human life. It is here that we immediately think of the Christian eschatological symbols of the Kingdom of God and the Communion of Saints, which powerfully reinforce the impetus to work for a perfected human society under God. As noted already, these concepts have inspired and can inspire an unrealistic millenarianism. Conversely they have been and can be interpreted solely in other-worldly, transcendental terms, deflecting attention from urgent present needs. And they have been and can be overlaid by individualistic conceptions of the vision of God, which have more in common with the solitary path. But there is no denying the influence of the dominant eschatological symbols in current Christian theology of hope, political theology and theology of liberation. We have already referred to dangers and excesses in these approaches, but, even so, the relation between Christian eschatology and social ethical concern is very close, just because of the social nature of the way in which the goal of human life is symbolised. It is not surprising to find that, in the posthumously published final fragments of his *Church Dogmatics*, Karl Barth was expounding the clause of the Lord's Prayer, 'Thy Kingdom come', under the heading '*fiat justitia*' – let justice be.[19]

The student of comparative religious ethics, especially if concentrating on potentialities for future development, will want to know how far it is possible for Buddhism and Hinduism to develop the eschatological and future-orientated strands that can be discerned in their visions of an ideal

---

[18] See K. Barth, *Church Dogmatics*, III/2, Edinburgh 1960, and III/4, Edinburgh 1961.

[19] See K. Barth, *The Christian Life*, Edinburgh 1981, pp. 260–271.

society, strands such as the use made in Mahayana Buddhism, of the eschatological figure of Maitreya, the Buddha-to-be, and the use within modern Hinduism of evolutionary ideas by Sri Aurobindo. We shall want to know how far such ideas can come to inspire and enable a dynamic social ethical concern.

Let me draw this chapter to a close by returning to its title theme – individual or social? – and summing up the tentative conclusions reached. It seems that there are good reasons for thinking that, however differently expressed in Buddhism, Christianity and Hinduism, it is a characteristically religious insight that the evil afflicting humanity will not finally be overcome without deep penetration within the human spirit to the level where ignorance is dispelled, craving ceases, sin is forgiven and estrangement from the ground of being done away with. The religions also have much to say, and increasingly more to say, about social justice and social transformation, but they are agreed in teaching that no external reordering of social life can hope to solve the human predicament, if the inner world of the spirit remains unhealed. To that extent, religion is peculiarly concerned with the individual. But two considerations lead us to qualify this judgement. The first is brought out by the asking how integral to the betterment of the individual the religions regard the betterment of human society to be. Here we have noted considerable differences both within each religion and between the three religions under discussion. Christianity, it appears, most obviously contains the conceptuality and indeed the dynamic for fostering radical social ethical concern. But it is extremely interesting to observe that, despite the factors noted in traditional Buddhism and Hinduism militating against such an active social concern, there are definite steps in the same direction within those religious faiths today. The more eschatological forms of Mahayana Buddhism, the bodhisattva ideal of compassionate concern for all suffering beings, and the reinterpretation of central Buddhist concepts in the sense of Buddhist socialism, are indications of this trend in Buddhism. Certain forms of Hindu *bhakti* religion and the renaissance and reform movements in nineteenth and twentieth-century Hinduism, including the emergence of personalistic humanism within Hinduism, are indications of this trend in Hinduism. How far these movements will come to prevail – and to prevail humanely – in Buddhist and Hindu cultures remains, of course, an open question.

In the second place we have to press the question, whether it is right to hold that the betterment of society comes about only through the betterment of individuals. Here the challenge of Marxism to the religions is at its most powerful. For despite the religions' strong objections to Marxist collectivism, abuse of power and neglect of the spiritual dimension, it surely does not follow that the transformation of society must wait upon the transformation of individuals. In fact, of course, the religions have always been aware of this. Traditional Buddhist, Christian and Hindu social ethics have involved commitment to a certain ordering of society, irrespective of the religion or the irreligion of the individual members of the society in question. But their religious priorities have traditionally lain elsewhere. What we are now invited to consider is whether the quest for social justice in fact belongs to the heart of man's religious quest, in such a way that it becomes impossible to follow the inward spiritual path without pursuing the outward path of work for social transformation too – as a matter of equal priority. And it is a characteristic of many modern versions of religious social ethics to see the task of constructing a better world not as something to be achieved indirectly only through the spiritual transformation of individuals, but as something to be worked for directly, politically, and in co-operation with all men and women of good will. Moreover, as we shall see in the final chapter, spirituality itself is increasingly understood to involve this social dimension. In theistic terms, God is encountered and discerned at work not only in the human heart, but also in the neighbour's need and in the movements for social justice in our time. The religions will, of course, maintain the equal priority of the individual's access to the world of the spirit. When that dimension is lost or played down, religion has indeed forsaken its special function and society has lost its soul. Moreover, *God* will hardly be discerned in the neighbour's need if he has not already been discerned in the heart. But it is a striking fact that many voices today, not only Christian but Buddhist and Hindu too, are claiming, admittedly with differing degrees of emphasis and plausibility, as we have seen, an equal centrality for social justice as a matter of essential religious concern. The heart of the problem, then, for the religions, is coming to be seen as both individual *and* social.

12

Religious resources for the overcoming of evil

Our first task in this final chapter is to consider a number of resources which the religions have held to be available to humankind toward the overcoming of evil. Deliberately, we will speak for the most part of these resources in human terms. Specifically religious resources are, of course, informed by religious beliefs, including, in some contexts, belief that it is God's grace and providence and action that are at work. But it is notoriously difficult, as Ninian Smart has pointed out, to differentiate between the effect of God's action in the world and the effect of belief in God's action in the world. And in any case in most theistic religions, human energies, including human beliefs, are held to be the vehicles or media of divine action.

One more preliminary point: the religions certainly have much to say about the ultimate overcoming of evil in a transcendent or ultimate eschatological state. Little will be said about that here. Our concern is with the religious resources for the overcoming of evil here and now or in the historical future.

We begin by mentioning education as a resource for the overcoming of evil; then, at rather greater length, we will examine the resources of spirituality. Under that heading, we will consider, in turn, meditation, asceticism and mysticism. We will be particularly interested in the question whether these modes of spirituality can yield a dynamic and effective social ethic. We will then ask the same question of prayer and devotional religion and belief in God's grace and, especially incarnation. Finally in this first part of the chapter we will attempt to compare and contrast the religious ideals of love, compassion and non-violence as resources in religious social ethics for the overcoming of evil.

In the second part of the chapter, we will consider very briefly the application of these resources to a number of specific problem areas in which we may discern the major social evils of our time. In asking how the religious resources previously identified can contribute to the overcoming of these ills, we are clearly only going to be able to sketch a programme for study.

I

We begin with *education*, because one ought not to lose sight of the fact that education has been and is one of the most important human resources for the overcoming of evil, nor of the fact that the religions have, over the centuries, contributed greatly to the cause of education in the world. Of course, much depends on *what* is taught. But it is widely and rightly held that the dispelling of ignorance and the acquisition of knowledge enable people to transcend the limitations of the situations in which they find themselves and contribute to making the world a better place. Among the things that can be taught is religious knowledge; and one hopes that religious education will open up the spiritual dimension of human existence and equip people at least with the possibility of drawing on specifically religious resources. We cannot enter into the vast territory of debate about religious education here. It is enough to point out that education, including religious education, can involve the imparting of wisdom and spirituality within a given social system, or it can lead to some radical challenge to that system and to pressure for social change. Much traditional religious education promoted individual virtue, stable family life and altruistic social service within the given order. But one has only to think of Swami Vivekananda, with his conviction that education in the principles of the Vedanta would rouse the Indian masses and enable them to take power, or of liberation theologians in

Latin America, with their programme of 'conscientisation', designed to awaken the people to the possibilities of sweeping change, to realise that education, as well as being a resource for making things better within the system, can also become a resource towards the transformation of society.

Religious rather than secular examples of this more radical use of education are deliberately mentioned here, since our purpose is to focus attention on such questions as whether religion, in its most characteristic aspects, itself requires and energises pressure for social change. This leads us immediately to pass on to consider spirituality and in what sense or senses spirituality can be thought of as a resource for the overcoming of evil.

It is not easy to find a definition of *spirituality* that does justice to both Eastern and Western spirituality and to both the classical traditions of Buddhist, Christian and Hindu spirituality and their developments and transformations in the modern age. The editor of the *Dictionary of Christian Spirituality*,[1] in his own article on 'Spirituality' tells us that the word has come to mean 'those attitudes, beliefs, practices which animate people's lives and help them to reach out towards supersensible realities'. Certainly, when people speak of the need to recover the dimension of the spirit, they seem to have in mind those levels of reality and experience to which we gain access by meditation, prayer, faith, or devotion, and which are held to yield different attitudes to life and different styles and modes of action from those usually characterised, by contrast, as materialistic or ideological.

We have a particular interest in enquiring into the relevance of spirituality to social and political action. It will be apparent from the last two chapters that much depends on the system of beliefs in which the traditions and paths of spirituality are embedded. The value accorded to interpersonal relationships and to society as such is bound to affect the forms and ideals of spirituality itself. From the viewpoint of social ethics we can understand suspicion of forms of spirituality which take a purely inward, individualistic path

[1] G. S. Wakefield (ed.), *A Dictionary of Christian Spirituality*, London 1983.

away from or above the world, society or even good and evil. But we saw reason not to be too hasty in setting the inward spiritual path against the outward path of social action. For people need enlightenment, salvation, liberation from the passions, ignorances and selfishnesses which mar all kinds of social system, which often cause great evils in the course of social transformation and which still corrupt and stain even the most seemingly just and equal human society. It may well be that the effect of spirituality is necessarily indirect. This is very probably what people have in mind when they say that we need to recover the dimension of spirituality. They perceive that spiritual qualities such as detachment, tranquillity and inner peace, especially if productive of, or accompanied by, compassion, truth-force or love, will act as powerful brakes on egoism, materialism, lust for power, the abuse of power and other dehumanising forces in the world. Such a view by itself, we note, involves endorsement of the idea that the world and society at large are bettered only through the betterment of individuals. We saw some reason to question this idea in the last chapter and we shall return to it below.

Perhaps the suspicion which, from the standpoint of social ethical concern, has been voiced about the concentration, in classical spirituality, East and West, on the interior life reflects not so much the fear that social evils are thereby at worst ignored or at best remedied only indirectly and very gradually, but rather the sense that the inner path is being allowed to monopolise the specifically religious dimension. Once again this is not just a practical question, but a matter of the interrelation of practice and belief. For the manner in which the dimension of spirituality is opened up depends on where one thinks the religious object is to be found. In theistic terms, it matters to one's understanding of spirituality whether one believes that God is to be found primarily within – in the cave of the heart – or whether God is equally, or even primarily, as some have urged, to be found in the ethical demands of the neighbour's need. It is unlikely that there is a strict either/or here. As pointed out in the last chapter, one will hardly find God in the poor and the oppressed if one's heart and soul have not been penetrated and moved by God deep within.

The Japanese Christian theologian, Kosume Koyama, in an article on 'Asian Spirituality',[2] differentiates very interestingly between Chinese, Indian and Japanese spirituality, embedded as each is in its respective culture. But despite these differentiations, he thinks it possible to discern a common basic pattern in Asian spirituality of what he calls cosmological spirituality by contrast with what he calls the eschatological spirituality of the West. The former is at home in cyclical views of the cosmos, sees human beings as part of nature as a whole and seeks the fundamental reality or truth underlying all there is. The latter confronts human beings and their world with a word, a judgement, a future hope, an ultimate transformation. Such a typology might lead us to suggest, as Robinson and Smart do,[3] the need for complementarity. The world needs both the social dynamism of eschatological spirituality and the inner integration of cosmological spirituality. There is much truth in this, although we have also stressed the need to see how far Hinduism and Buddhism themselves are developing dynamic social ethics out of their own resources. But if one needs both eschatological and cosmological spirituality, one has to be alert to the dangers of each type when developed to an extreme. The danger of allowing eschatological spirituality to develop too far in the direction of radicalism is that of a religious activism which finds God only in the needs of the poor and the oppressed. This way spirituality tends to evaporate into ideology. The danger of allowing cosmological spirituality to locate the meeting-point of the religions solely in 'the cave of the heart' is that of ignoring the religious dimension to the cry for social justice.

It might appear that more stress has been laid here on the latter danger than on the former; and it is true that in what follows about meditation, asceticism and mysticism, this latter danger will be held very much in mind. But the former danger is equally serious. As we have seen, the religions' quarrel with Marxism is precisely over the dehumanising nature of

---

[2] K. Koyama, 'Asian Spirituality', *A Dictionary of Christian Spirituality*, pp. 29–32.
[3] J. A. T. Robinson, *Truth is Two-Eyed*, London 1979; and N. Smart, *Beyond Ideology*, London 1981.

precipitate, ideologically based, action that ignores the spiritual needs of people and overlooks the corruptions of power. Religiously motivated social action must avoid such traps if it is to remain religious. It is a matter of religious perception that evil cannot be overcome by evil.

We turn, then to consider *prayer* and *meditation* as religious resources for the overcoming of evil. Again the effectiveness for good of ordinary men and women of prayer in every religious tradition should not be underestimated. Moreover, there are striking parallels between the religions both at lowly and at higher levels of mental prayer and meditation, as Thomas Merton found in the course of his Asian journey.[4] The meditations of the Buddhist and the Christian monk may have had different content, but the effect in penetration through to levels of non-attachment and dispassion is very similar. Not only are the inner evils of craving, passion and selfishness dispelled by these means, but such disciplines yield fruit in terms of the virtues, gentleness, tranquillity, compassion, love. More will be said of these virtues – and about their similarities and differences – below. But clearly they contribute to the overcoming of evil in the world.

We should also consider the criticisms of these spiritual techniques that have been voiced. Detachment can become an end in itself. But something has surely gone wrong if exalted mental states are cultivated for their own sake rather than for their fruits in qualities of life and action. This seems to be at the root of suspicions expressed by many Christians at the vogue for 'transcendental meditation', which has made a considerable impact in the West. As a technique for achieving deep relaxation, this can clearly be of benefit to over-busy people in the modern world. One thinks of Dag Hammarskjöld's advocacy of meditation not least for politicians, and his insistence on provision of a meditation room at the headquarters of the United Nations in New York. But the problem with detachment is that one can become detached not only from craving, passion and worry, but also from the needs of other people and of society at large. We can

[4] See N. Burton, et al. (eds.), *The Asian Journal of Thomas Merton*, London 1974.

understand the Marxists' impatience with the channelling of the mind's energies into apparently unproductive states. Do we not rather need a passionate concern for social justice? On the other hand, even transcendental meditation can be defended if its techniques are used to release energies for social service and making the world a better place. The techniques may be neutral. It all depends on the system of commitments in relation to which they are used.

Moreover, when we remember what harm can be done by intemperate ideologically motivated activists, riding roughshod over human beings in the interests of some abstract ideal of justice, we begin to see the point of a middle way between the extremes of detachment and activism. Religion may be seen to provide the resources of dispassionate concern and a commitment to one's fellow human beings which nevertheless is not prepared to sacrifice the few for the many, let alone the many for the many. It is clear that the Buddha's teaching, the Sermon on the Mount and the Bhagavadgita all, in their different ways, commend and enable such dispassionate concern.

Our interest in religious social ethics may obscure the fact that values other than ethical values – specifically religious values – are at stake in spiritual practices such as meditation. There are undoubtedly purely religious values, just as there are purely aesthetic values. And human life is the poorer for the neglect of these values. Moreover it is no more selfish to dedicate oneself to the pursuit of religious truth than to dedicate oneself to artistic creativity. A case can be made for the view that the world is a better place where both purely religious and artistic values are accorded their due significance. Social ethical concern is not the only matter of importance for religious men and women. Perhaps, after all, there is a sense in which it is right to pursue the path of meditation for its own sake.

But it remains the case that the religions are finding more and more that social ethical concern cannot be bypassed or transcended in the interests of some higher goal. There may be other religious values, but they are not higher values, and it is a matter of considerable interest as well as of importance to see how all the religions are incorporating this truth into their value systems. We see this in Mahayana Buddhism in the bodhisattva who postpones his own enlightenment for the sake of suffering humanity. We see it in Christianity in the discernment of Christ's presence in the poor and the hungry as much as in the stillness of mental prayer. We see it in Hinduism in Radhakrishnan's insistence that 'we cannot lose ourselves in inner piety when the poor die at our doors, naked and hungry'.[5] Our only query concerns the degree to which each religion's characteristic beliefs help their development to take place.

Similar remarks may be made about asceticism and about mysticism as resources for the overcoming of evil. Where *asceticism* is concerned, all the religions have seen the need for self-discipline if spiritual goals are to be attained. But much depends on what those spiritual goals are held to be and also on beliefs about the significance of the body. The danger of extreme asceticism for its own sake has been clearly recognised. It was deliberately renounced by the Buddha in his Middle Way; and the solitary ascetism of the early desert fathers in Christianity was eventually repudiated in favour of monastic community discipline, which itself came under rather extreme inner-Christian criticism at the time of the Reformation, though, ideally, monastic communities are supposed to exist for the sake of the Church and the world. Twentieth-century Christianity has seen, to a large extent, the rejection of the soul–body dualism which encouraged ascetic practices and a positive appraisal of the body as God's good creation. It is not clear whether the Hindu ascetic practices so vividly described by Klaus Klostermaier in his *Hindu and Christian in Vrindaban*[6] are universally or widely repudiated in Hinduism today, but one notes that S. N. Dasgupta, already in the 1920s, was endorsing the Buddha's rejection of any quasi-magical view of the powers acquired through extreme self-mortification.[7] Not all Hindu asceticism is of that kind, of course. But from the viewpoint of social ethical concern, the

[5] S. Radhakrishnan, *Eastern Religion and Western Thought*, London 1939, p. 109.
[6] K. Klostermaier, *Hindu and Christian in Vrindaban*, London 1969.
[7] S. Dasgupta, *Hindu Mysticism*, New York 1927, ch. IV.

solitary ascetic in any religion is bound to be an object of some suspicion.

Mysticism is a much more positive phenomenon and a major factor in the history of religions. It is not possible here to analyse its different forms or to debate the question whether mysticism is fundamentally the same phenomenon, though interpreted differently in the different religions. Without denying the value of mystical experience as such, we may stress the importance of the framework of belief in terms of which it is interpreted. The mystic may have overcome evil in himself and as it impinges upon him as an individual, but whether he becomes a source of wider amelioration for other people depends on how he understands his mystical experience. It makes a difference whether he feels himself to be caught up to a transcendent plane beyond and above all distinctions, or whether he feels himself to be united with a love that permeates and energises all created beings. One might refer here to Ursula King's *Towards a New Mysticism*,[8] subtitled 'Teilhard de Chardin and Eastern Religions', in which she develops Teilhard's account of mysticism as 'culminating in a radiant centre of energy and love linked to a dynamic mysticism of action'. There is the possibility of a convergence of traditions here. As King says in her epilogue, the greatest religious problem today is how to combine the search for an expansion of inner awareness with effective social action, and how to find one's true identity in the synthesis of both.

Suspicion of mysticism without love leads us to consider more directly the contributions of *devotional religion* to the overcoming of evil. The resources of worship and the love of God are among the most obvious and widespread of religious resources for the overcoming of evil; and through them God's grace and providence are held to work for the good of all. It has to be admitted that in every religion many dubious or false beliefs are bound up with devotional practices directed to the overcoming of evil. Demonological beliefs are an obvious example. But for all the variety and often

[8] U. King, *Towards a New Mysticism*, London 1980, p. 216.

implausibility of popular religious belief about the nature, causes and remedies of evil and suffering, it remains the case that this is the level at which the so-called consolations of religion operate for the majority of believers. Devotional religion has also inspired a great deal of love and compassion, not only at the level of such saintly figures as that of Mother Teresa of Calcutta, but also at much more lowly levels of service and care. Belief in divine providence and grace and in divine incarnation has inspired and enabled social action and involvement in a world understood to be the sphere of God's own care and active concern. Thus it was in the context of Christian incarnational theology that the Social Gospel and Christian Socialism were developed in England, Germany and America in the late nineteenth and early twentieth centuries. Our interest in comparable developments in Buddhism and Hinduism has already led us to refer, in the previous chapter, to Buddhist socialism and its justification by appeal to certain key Buddhist doctrines, and to the Ramakrishna Mission and the Sarvodaya movement in Hinduism. Hinduism, of course, contains a fascinating parallel to the Christian doctrine of the Incarnation in the Avatar doctrines of Vaishnavism.[9] In the Gita, Krishna says that God incarnates himself in order to preserve *dharma* whenever wickedness is flourishing. But even modern interpretations of the Gita recognise that its positive ethical teaching is still coloured by the older idea of detachment. G. W. Kaveeshwar, for example, describes the ideal person as one who has achieved a state of absolute equanimity, who acts as occasion demands totally dispassionately. 'Otherwise absorbed in spiritual meditation, he will remain perfectly content within himself.'[10] It may seem rather surprising that this ideal inspired Mahatma Gandhi to involve himself in the plight of the outcastes and the victims of colonialism. But clearly the idea that one must act where necessary in the prevailing circumstances is susceptible of wider or narrower application. On the face of it, though, there seems little impulse here for going beyond what is necessary

---

[9] See G. Parrinder, *Avatar and Incarnation*, London 1970.
[10] G. W. Kaveeshwar, *The Ethics of the Gita*, Delhi 1971, p. 240.

in the interests of other people. On this score, Mahayana Buddhism, with its bodhisattva ideal of compassionate work for suffering humanity and its conviction of the saving grace of Amida Buddha, seems closer to Christian incarnational religion, though again the culmination of the Christian story of the Incarnation in the way of the cross is indicative of important differences as well.

This leads us to consider love, compassion and non-violence as ideals and resources for the overcoming of evil. There is room for a great deal of careful and detailed comparative work here. On the one hand, there can be no doubt that these spiritual resources and ideals, fostered by the three religions with which we are concerned, have made the world a much better place than it would have been without them. Countless self-sacrificial lives and acts have been inspired by and have exemplified these virtues. Much evil has been overcome by them. On the other hand, the differences between these virtues and the differences in the styles of life and modes of action which flow from them should not be ignored.

The virtue of *love*, as understood in the Christian tradition, has been subjected to detailed analysis in contemporary Christian ethics in such books as Gene Outka's *Agape*,[11] and, in smaller compass, James Gustafson's *Can Ethics be Christian?*[12] One thing becomes clear from such studies, namely, the variety of ways in which Christian love has been understood in Christian ethics. Anyone approaching the matter from outside and reading only Anders Nygren's *Agape and Eros*[13] would gain a very misleading impression of what love means in the Christian tradition. For, although altruistic love, including active love of the sick, the poor and the oppressed, and including love of the unlovely and of the enemy, has certainly characterised the Christian ideal, based as it is on God's love revealed and embodied in Christ's love, it has seldom, been set as starkly as by Nygren in opposition to a proper self-love and a proper and disciplined desire for

---

[11] G. Outka, *Agape*, New Haven, Conn. 1972.
[12] J. M. Gustafson, *Can Ethics be Christian?*, Chicago 1975.
[13] A. Nygren, *Agape and Eros*, London 1953.

the beloved object. Indeed the Augustinian tradition in Christianity, far from treating all desire as evil, has seen in humanity's desire for God a mark of our true nature and destiny. And even the enemy and the unlovely are not loved irrespective of their status and destiny as children of God and fellow-heirs with Christ. Furthermore, just because Christianity teaches a relational conception of God as *being* love, and a social conception of the ultimate destiny of men and women in the communion of saints, Christian love has an undeniable social dimension. It inspires and demands the quest for justice. Indeed, as mentioned in chapter 5, a Christian exponent of situation ethics, Joseph Fletcher, for whom the love principle is the only absolute principle of action, has asserted that 'justice is love distributed'.[14] It should be added that Christian love, inspired and enabled by the love of God revealed and enacted in the life and passion of Christ, will be liable in a wicked world to manifest just those qualities of self-sacrifice, involving redemptive suffering and vicarious suffering, that we see most clearly in the Cross of Christ. That remains the pattern and the paradigm of Christian love.

Similar studies, in depth, are urgently required of the Buddhist ideal of *karuna* or compassion. As mentioned already, we would want to ask what difference it makes that it has as its object the good of all living creatures, not simply humans, and that its aim is to help all living beings to enter the city of Nirvana. We would need to press the question how active a concern is universal friendliness or *metta*, with which *karuna* is closely associated in Buddhist teaching. Can this Buddhist ideal foster and sustain commitment to social justice? Paul Tillich once wrote, 'participation leads to agape, identity to compassion'.[15] Can this contrast be made out? The question has already been raised how far the no-self doctrine affects the nature of Buddhist compassion. We would also need to press the question how far the Buddhist ideal of compassion mirrors and is enabled by a divine paradigm. Certain developments in Mahayana Buddhism, such as the

[14] J. Fletcher, *Situation Ethics*, London 1966. See p. 72 above.
[15] P. Tillich, *Christianity and the Encounter of World Religions*, New York 1963, p. 70.

doctrine of the Amida Buddha's grace, indicate that this potentiality exists in Buddhism, though its centrality may be questioned. Vicarious suffering is certainly a feature of the budhisattva ideal, even if its redemptive purpose is not always stressed.

There is a considerable literature on the Hindu concept of *ahimsa.* One thinks particularly of the writings of Gandhi himself, and those of Vinoba Bhave. The Finnish scholar, Unto Tähtinen, has devoted a monograph to *Ahimsa: Non-violence in Indian Tradition,*[16] with reference to the Jains and the Buddhists as well as to classical and contemporary Hinduism. Gandhi's interpretation and deployment of this key concept in Indian thought is very striking. A central feature of it is non-exploitation. This has widely ramifying social, economic and political consequences. It is not just a negative characteristic. Wrongness is actively resisted by relentless dissociation from evil activities. As such *ahimsa* can be universal. *Ahimsa* is not the only virtue for Gandhi. Fearlessness and especially truthfulness are also taught. Indeed it could be said, that, for Gandhi, truth is the greatest in the hierarchy of virtues, as love was for St Paul.

It might be argued that this contrast between *ahimsa* and love has been overdrawn. After all, Gandhi did elsewhere speak of *ahimsa* as the greater love. Moreover Vivekananda had already set it in the context of the love of God. But striking contrasts may also be observed between the Christian teaching on love of God and love of neighbour and the following passage from Vivekananda's famous address at the World Parliament of Religions in Chicago in 1893:

> It is good to love God for hope of reward in this or the next world, but it is better to love God for love's sake . . . One of the disciples of Krishna, the then Emperor of India, was driven from his kingdom by his enemies and had to take shelter with his queen in a forest in the Himalayas, and there one day the queen asked him how it was that he, the most virtuous of men, should suffer so much misery. Yuddhishthira answered, 'Behold, my queen, the Himalayas, how grand and beautiful they are. I love them. They

[16] U. Tähtinen, *Ahimsa: Non-Violence in Indian Tradition,* London 1976.

do not give me anything, but my nature is to love the grand, the beautiful, therefore I love them. Similarly I love the Lord. He is the source of all beauty, of all sublimity. He is the only object to be loved, my nature is to love him, and therefore I love. I do not pray for anything; I do not ask for anything. Let Him place me wherever he likes, I must love Him for love's sake. I cannot trade in love.'[17]

This is a striking passage, but it manifests a different conception of love from that of agape.

To return to the topic of *ahisma* – the way in which its social, economic and political implications have been developed by Vinoba Bhave and the Sarvodaya movement show it to be a very powerful religious resource for the overcoming of social evil. It is debatable, however, whether it is powerful enough, whether, for example, it is realistic to expect land to be redistributed by voluntary gift. Vinoba Bhave held that Sarvodaya was more radical than Marxism and socialism because it sought to change not only social institutions but also the basic values of people in society. But in holding to the principle that society will be bettered only by the betterment of individuals, it underestimated the recalcitrance of institutional structures and also the possibility of responsible use of power. By contrast, Christian social ethics usually holds that love at times requires the responsible and disciplined constraint of others, just as Jesus himself drove the pigeon sellers from the Temple.

II

In the second section of this final chapter, we will briefly consider how specifically religious resources such as those just discussed might be applied to the problems of overcoming certain pervasive contemporary social evils.

We begin with the ecological crisis, which modern technology and its thoughtless use have brought upon the world. This is one of the most alarming effects of materialism, and of a growth-orientated consumer society. Christianity has often

---

[17] S. Vivekananda, *Chicago Addresses*, Calcutta, 19th impression 1980, pp. 21f.

been accused of fostering this mentality by its Genesis-based doctrine of humanity's dominion over the earth, including the animals. To a certain extent Christian ethics can, from its own resources, put its own house in order on this matter. The responsible stewardship of nature is in fact more soundly based in the Christian tradition than dominion over nature, and Christian spirituality, exemplified in the life and writings of St Francis, can provide the basis for a reverent attitude to all God's creatures. But it is widely and rightly felt that the West has much to learn from the East about living in harmony with nature. As Kosuke Koyama puts it, 'in the time of brutal exploitation of nature, the cosmological piety is beginning to demonstrate its ecological conviction to humanity'.[18] At all events this is one of the clearest points at which a convergence of religious resources from East and West can help to form a climate of respect, even reverence, for the natural environment. An indication of the resources of the Vedanta for such a view may be found in an article by E. Deutsch, entitled 'Vedanta and Ecology',[19] in which he writes that, for Vedanta theory,

> nature . . . becomes infused with quality, with spiritual life, as well as with measurable processes . . . The core ideas . . . are that nature is interconnected, that there is a continuity between man and all other things, and that everything in nature, being an inseparable part of the whole and retaining its qualitative origin, has intrinsic value.

Similarly, as Ursula King brings out, it was Teilhard's dominant concern to discover and proclaim a new mysticism of communion with God through the earth.[20] But, while the cultivation of such attitudes to the environment is much to be desired, and while religious resources may indeed contribute to their formation, the problem is so great that only political will and political action, indeed international co-operative action, can hope to stem the tide of destruction and halt the rape of nature. The question then arises whether the religions

---

[18] K. Koyama, 'Asian Spirituality', *A Dictionary of Christian Spirituality*, p. 32.
[19] E. Deutsch, 'Vedanta and Ecology', *Indian Philosophical Annual*, 1971.
[20] King, *Towards a New Mysticism*, ch. 9.

can do more than just help to change attitudes and to form attitudes or whether it is not also a religious duty and task to engage, with all men and women of good will, in political action to halt the destruction and abuse of nature. Even on the question of ecological concern, therefore, we come up against the ethical imperative to do more than just seek to better the world through the betterment of individuals.

We turn next to the social evil of sexism and to the disparagement of sexuality in general, a topic on which, I fear, the religions have a most ambiguous record. This is true of all three religions with which we are concerned, which are in any case at very different stages of development on this matter. Moreover the historical interaction of religions began on a large scale at a time when Christianity was dominated by very puritanical attitudes to matters of sex and before the modern pressures for equality between the sexes had had much effect. The facts about the religions' attitudes to sex may be gleaned from Geoffrey Parrinder's *Sex in the World's Religions*,[21] and very varied and ambiguous they are. It takes much discrimination and some reinterpretation of Buddhist, Christian and Hindu ideas to locate the religious resources for overcoming the evils concerned with sex. Sexism, which usually means the disparagement and unequal treatment of women, is only one of those evils. Others are, of course, the trivialisation and exploitation of sex, but also its denigration and devaluation. Another evil widely felt, at least in the developed world, is the masculine domination of the language and imagery of religion itself. In an article on 'Feminine Spirituality', Nancy Ring indicates some of the religious resources for remedying the evil of the masculine domination of spirituality and for finding in specifically feminine responses something of universal import for spirituality.[22] Where the wider social issues are concerned, all three religions contain elements that can help to foster a high evaluation of the person as a sexual being, and as equal, irrespective of sexuality. Christians, at any rate, who have long proclaimed that 'in Christ there is neither

---

[21] G. Parrinder, *Sex in the World's Religions*, London 1980.
[22] N. Ring, 'Feminine Spirituality', *A Dictionary of Christian Spirituality*, pp. 148ff.

male nor female',[23] are now learning to appreciate the positive significance of both embodiment and sexuality in God's good creation, and to see in faithful, committed, sexual love an image and a sacrament of the divine love – a fact appreciated long ago by the author of the Song of Songs.

The evils of *war* need no elaboration. And, although, as acknowledged at the beginning of chapter 10, the religions can justly be accused of fomenting and exacerbating human strife at many points in their histories and still today, nevertheless there exist powerful spiritual resources in the Buddhist, Christian and Hindu traditions for overcoming these evils and for creating the conditions and sustaining the attitudes that make for peace.[24] Buddhism has some claim to be the most pacific of the great world religions. The first of the Five Precepts prohibits the taking of life, and the Noble Eightfold Path is explicitly designed to overcome the craving that expresses itself in resentment and hostility. Although addressed primarily to the individual, the Buddhist teaching and characteristic attitudes of gentleness and compassion have greatly affected Buddhist societies and Buddhist statesmen such as U Thant, the third Secretary General of the United Nations. The witness of Buddhist monks in Vietnam made a deep impression in the West, and for a time had a considerable effect on American foreign policy. Buddhists have been prominent in the peace movements evoked by the nuclear threat.

Something has already been said about the prominence of the idea of non-violence in modern Hinduism. Taken together the religions of the East, at their best, provide deeply pacific spiritual resources against the resort to war.

Christianity too, in essence, preaches a message of peace on earth, goodwill towards men. Jesus, in the Sermon on the Mount, taught non-resistance and extolled the peacemakers. The Christian gospel is a gospel of reconciliation, and, as we have already seen, Christian ethics treats love as the supreme virtue and principle of action. But, while Christian pacifism

---

[23] Galatians 3.28.
[24] For a brief survey of religious attitudes to war and peace, see J. Ferguson, *War and Peace in the World's Religions*, London 1977.

has a long and honoured history, for the greater part of the Christian centuries the Churches have endorsed just war theory, and in fact Christian nations have been extremely bellicose. It is not surprising that, second only to Islam, Christianity has been regarded as a factor making for war rather than for peace. In the period of the Cold War, under the threat of nuclear annihilation, Christians recovered, to some extent, their original gospel of peace on earth and made a marked contribution to peace movements on both sides of the then prevailing iron curtain. The head of the Campaign for Nuclear Disarmamant was, at that time, a Roman Catholic Monsignor, Bruce Kent. In fact, his position and attitude illustrate very well the question whether religious resources are aimed at the betterment of the world only through the betterment of individuals or also, more directly, through political action to remedy social evils. Kent clearly took the latter view. He said in an interview: 'the Gospel is there not just to set man free from sin, but from what sin has done to society.' For Kent, it was part of responsible Christian action, indeed of Christian spirituality, to work with men and women of any faith or none for nuclear disarmament. And presumably he saw God at work not only in the hearts of men and women to make them more peaceable but in the political pressure groups working for disarmament and peace. It is easy to criticise this view on the grounds that the attempt to apply the gospel message directly to the political ordering of society is a matter of very fallible judgement, involves a large number of sinful men and women, and has led in the past to inquisitions and wars of religion. And it may well be that Kent was wrong about the desirability of unilateral disarmament. But Christianity cannot withdraw the scope of its spiritual concerns to the cave of the heart alone. It needs the consciousness of fallibility. It needs self-criticism and the criticism of others, both religious and secular. But it cannot give up its biblically based conviction that God is at work not only in the human heart but in all that makes for peace and justice in God's world.

Mention of justice brings me to the last two social evils to be considered in connection with the question of religious resources for the overcoming of evil: *poverty* and *injustice*. There is not space here to do much more than mention these most crucial areas of social ethics and indicate the bearing of our previous considerations on the special contribution of the religions to the quest for social justice. We cannot deal with the way in which the voluntary embracing of poverty can itself become a religious value. The notions of 'holy poverty' and of the renunciation of wealth have a long history in religion, and we have already touched on this issue in speaking of asceticism. Again, the Incarnation, God's own self-emptying and identification with the poor, is a powerful theme in historical Christianity. And poverty is after all one of the three monastic vows. But we are thinking here of involuntary poverty, debilitating poverty, world poverty – social evils of monstrous proportions, which shame us all, especially in the West. Of course, the problems of poverty and injustice in the world are primarily political problems, and the religions as such have no easy panaceas to offer to the politicians. Indeed, for much of their histories, as we have seen, Buddhism, Christianity and Hinduism have offered, chiefly, on the one hand inner consolation, inner ways of liberation and escape, and on the other hand, no more than benevolence and charity to the victims of these social ills. But we have noted how all three religions in the modern period have come to see it as their *religious* duty to work, politically, for social justice. We have seen how Buddhist, Christian and Hindu teachings are, in differing degrees, being reinterpreted to demand egalitarian policies and a fairer social and economic order. We have already referred to Buddhist socialism, Christian liberation theology, and to the Hindu Sarvodaya movement. Desmond Tutu in South Africa and David Sheppard in England have alike endorsed the 'bias to the poor' which Christianity requires of the Churches in the field of social ethics.[25] But what special resource do the religions bring to these concerns, which are after all the sphere of much secular political action, both nationally and internationally?

[25] See D. Sheppard, *Bias to the Poor*, London 1983.

If the movements stressed in these last three chapters are any guide, it cannot simply be a matter of religion and spirituality checking the passions and teaching us to respect the humanity of all caught up in processes of social change. On the contrary, the domain of spirituality has been discovered itself to extend into the sphere of social ethics and the quest or struggle for justice. Religiously inspired compassion, non-violence and love all require and enable a deeper and certainly more humane involvement in building what the World Council of Churches calls a 'just, participatory, and sustainable society'. What makes spirituality both radical and a powerful force for social reform is undoubtedly the insight that it is there in the needs of the poor and the oppressed that God is especially to be found. God is also to be found in the heights and depths of contemplation, and, as already suggested, it may well be that God will not be recognised in the cry of the oppressed for justice, if he has not already been found in the cave of the heart. But, in drawing these chapters on the overcoming of evil to a close, we can only re-emphasise the fact that all the world religions, not just Christianity, are now finding themselves drawn to apply the resources of spirituality to the political as well as to the individual task of making the world a better place.

Index